Low-Fat Love Stories

Yvette —
I hope you enjoy!

Love and Light,

Patricia

Social Fictions Series

Series Editor
Patricia Leavy
USA

The *Social Fictions* series emerges out of the arts-based research movement. The series includes full-length fiction books that are informed by social research but written in a literary/artistic form (novels, plays, and short story collections). Believing there is much to learn through fiction, the series only includes works written entirely in the literary medium adapted. Each book includes an academic introduction that explains the research and teaching that informs the book as well as how the book can be used in college courses. The books are underscored with social science or other scholarly perspectives and intended to be relevant to the lives of college students—to tap into important issues in the unique ways that artistic or literary forms can.

Please email queries to pleavy7@aol.com

Low-Fat Love Stories

Patricia Leavy and Victoria Scotti

SENSE PUBLISHERS
ROTTERDAM/BOSTON/TAIPEI

A C.I.P. record for this book is available from the Library of Congress.

ISBN: 978-94-6300-816-7 (paperback)
ISBN: 978-94-6300-817-4 (hardback)
ISBN: 978-94-6300-818-1 (e-book)

Published by: Sense Publishers,
P.O. Box 21858,
3001 AW Rotterdam,
The Netherlands
https://www.sensepublishers.com/

All chapters in this book have undergone peer review.

Cover art and design by Victoria Scotti

The backgrounds of the portraits in this book were created using Stampers Anonymous stencils. Used with permission © Stampers Anonymous, http://www.stampersanonymous.com/

Printed on acid-free paper

PRAISE FOR
LOW-FAT LOVE STORIES

"A powerful book that explores the effect of living in the context of a commercial culture that tells women they are not enough. Through both the stories and portraits, *Low-Fat Love Stories* challenges the representations of women that dominate popular culture, offering alternative narratives and images grounded in women's real experiences. This will be an engaging springboard for self and social reflection in classes."
– Sut Jhally, Ph.D., University of Massachusetts at Amherst; Founder & Executive Director, Media Education Foundation

"*Low-Fat Love Stories* is wonderful! I love it. The images are glorious – emotionally compelling – those eyes, the pain, the fragility; the stories are captivating. The combination of visual images, handwritten journal entries, and stories captures the anguish and hope of women extraordinarily well. Each "textual-visual snapshot" takes you on a breathtaking journey. The methodology is original, exciting, and compelling. I am a writer and a visual artist. Bringing together the two modes has been a life-long challenge for me. Hurrah! This book models a way for me to at long last integrate my creative expressions. I think it will do that for others. I highly recommend *Low-Fat Love Stories* for general readers, book clubs, writing groups, and any number of college courses."
– Laurel Richardson, Ph.D., Professor Emeritus, The Ohio State University and Cooley Book Award winner

"*Low-Fat Love Stories* places women's experiences and words at the forefront. Through visual art and stories, this book challenges the representations of women we typically see in popular culture and offers alternatives. An important addition to the fields of gender and media studies that is certain to stimulate self-reflection and lively discussion."
– Jean Kilbourne, Ed.D., author, feminist activist, and creator of the *Killing Us Softly: Advertising's Image of Women* film series

"A wonderful model of the infinite possibilities for art as research where conversations with fifty-six women are distilled and transformed into one compelling work proving that artistic expression is uniquely capable of offering transparent evidence and honest insights into complex human conditions. The book shows how fiction as a psychological medium can go where standard psychological formats simply cannot go in getting close to intimate experience. Text and drawings communicate the "dark truth" and make it into an inspirational affirmation of life for all people."
– Shaun McNiff, Ph.D., University Professor, Lesley University and author of *Art as Research*, *Art Heals*, and *Imagination in Action*

"Leavy's words and Scotti's images transform intimate interviews into captivating portraits of the unspoken inner lives of women – bringing to life the source of their insecurities and fears, and staying alongside these women as they find the courage and strength to change their circumstances. This is important reading for those who've experienced similar, and everyone who wants to better understand what is left invisible. A timely read for a growing national conversation."
– Nick Sousanis, Ph.D., Assistant Professor, San Francisco State University and award-winning author of *Unflattening*

"Powerful and riveting! *Low-Fat Love Stories* captures women's struggles with self-esteem in very real and visceral ways through "textual-visual snapshots." This innovative, collaborative practice between an author and a visual artist facilitates a uniquely conceptualized methodology that stretches our impressions and encourages women to reimagine their lives. Most importantly, women's lives count! This collection of stories resonates with the experiences of all women and will assuredly benefit all women, and yes, the men in their lives."
– Rita L. Irwin, Ph.D., Professor and Associate Dean of Teacher Education, The University of British Columbia

"*Low-Fat Love Stories* is anything but low-fat. This gorgeous book is full of music; the images and stories of women's relational lives will resonate long after you experience them. This work represents the best of arts-based research, collaborative work, and feminist research. It questions the damaging popular discourse that romance means happily ever after and that romance is women's biggest achievement. I intend to buy this for all the women and men in my life."
– Sandra L. Faulkner, Ph.D., Director of Women's, Gender, and Sexuality Studies, Bowling Green State University and coauthor of *Writing the Personal*

"With this collection of *Low-Fat Love Stories*, Leavy and Scotti continue to expand curriculum and strategies for teaching arts-and-research. *Low-Fat Love Stories* is also an excellent text for teaching education and sociology courses about gender, sexuality, and popular culture. Best of all, *Low-Fat Love Stories* is a great read and a joy for lay readers, instructors, and students alike."
– Susan Finley, Ph.D., Professor, Washington State University and acclaimed arts author and activist

"*Low-Fat Love Stories* takes readers on a journey into women's hearts, minds, bodies and relationships that is by turns heartbreaking, realistic, difficult, and inspirational. The stories and artwork ask women to consider how they can love, nurture, and grow in their work and their relationships in ways that resist and revise the seemingly endless stream of images and messages that devalue and demean us. In a time when women are shamed, blamed, violated, and told they deserve less, *Low-Fat Love Stories* tells a new kind of fairy tale: one in which women are powerful, smart, beautiful, and in charge of their own lives and loves."
– Stacy Holman Jones, Ph.D., Professor, Monash University and coauthor of *Writing for Performance* and *Autoethnography: Understanding Qualitative Research*

"Leavy and Scotti use interviews, techniques of fiction, and stunning visual art to identify and critique prominent cultural fairytales, problematic portrayals of women in popular culture, and unrealistic expectations about love. They also show how women might live through/with toxic relationships, abuse, aging, body image dissatisfaction, and (not) loving themselves. Methodologically and topically, *Low-Fat Love Stories* makes a noteworthy contribution to both gender and arts-based research."
– Tony E. Adams, Ph.D., Associate Professor, Northeastern Illinois University and award-winning author of *Narrating the Closet*

"In this deeply innovative work, Leavy and Scotti use visual art and story-telling to represent women's lived experiences of "low-fat love." Heartbreaking, raw, and beautifully executed, their unique approach to the doing of social science research will inspire scholars to further push the boundaries of what research might look like, and how it might touch and influence others."
– Jessica Smartt Gullion, Ph.D., Interim Assistant Dean of the College of Arts and Sciences, Texas Woman's University

"In *Low-Fat Love Stories*, we are found in each other's stories and enter the syllables of our own becoming. Leavy and Scotti call us to honor both vulnerability and strength, and the ability to recreate a life, not hindered by patterns or limitations of one's own perceptions. By integrating an arts-based practice and weaving textual-visual snapshots, the stories of the women in this book, catch us in an earthy and radiant tone, and we are beckoned to boldly live and celebrate our authentic lives."
– Celeste Snowber, Ph.D., Associate Professor, Simon Fraser University and author of *Embodied Prayer* and *Embodied Inquiry*

Also from Patricia Leavy

Blue

Low-Fat Love: Expanded Anniversary Edition

Gender & Pop Culture: A Text-Reader
Edited by Adrienne Trier-Bieniek and Patricia Leavy

For more information, visit the author's website
www.patricialeavy.com

*This book is dedicated to the remarkable women
who bravely shared their stories with us.
We are grateful for their candor, wisdom and honesty.*

TABLE OF CONTENTS

PREFACE

Low-Fat Love, my debut novel, was released in 2011. I never intended to write a novel, nor could I have anticipated the response.

Over the course of almost a decade I had conducted interview research with about five hundred women and nearly a hundred men about their relationships, body image issues, and identities. I was struck by patterns that emerged across many of the women's interviews. While I never asked women directly about a negative relationship experience, that's what many chose to talk about. I believe this is because women are rarely afforded the opportunity to talk freely about these experiences that fly in the face of idealistic cultural romance and family narratives. Many also spoke about struggles with self-esteem which manifested in various ways, including negative relationship experiences with romantic partners, friends, relatives, and others, as well as dissatisfaction with their bodies or their overall appearance.

During this time I was also teaching undergraduate sociology courses about gender, sexuality, and popular culture. These courses included ample discussion, usually with us sitting in a circle. During my office hours, students often shared their personal experiences. I began to develop cumulative insights based on both my interviewees and these conversations with students, both inside and outside of class. For example, I noticed that many women spoke about themselves relationally and seemed to have a difficult time talking about themselves outside of the context of relationships. Women also frequently told me about their daily body image struggles, even those who first claimed to be "fine." Overall, what struck me in all of these stories was how many women were grappling with self-esteem issues in private, and how many seemed to be settling in life and love, with dissatisfaction brewing beneath the surface. Sometimes they tried to save face by backtracking in their narratives, telling me that things were better than they may seem. I was dubious. As their professor or interviewer, I wasn't in a position to offer candid advice, which would have been inappropriate. This left me frustrated.

I also identified with many of these women. When I was younger, I too suffered from self-esteem issues and settled in various areas of life, including toxic romantic relationships. Through my work and sustained reflection about my own role in shaping my life through the choices I was making, I developed a radically altered sense of self and changed my life for the better.

In search of a way to capture what I had been learning, I developed the concept of "low-fat love," which refers to settling for less than we want and trying to pretend it is better than it is (Leavy, 2011, 2015). We may be able to fake ourselves out with a diet cookie, at least for a while, but when it comes to how we feel about ourselves and our intimate others, faking it doesn't work. Diet relationships fail, and leave us longing for more. People settle for low-fat love in different kinds of relationships, for various reasons: they don't think they deserve more, can get more, and will get more, or they don't recognize they're settling until they are frustrated, disappointed, or discontent and they may not even know why. This is all occurring in a cultural context in which there's a highly limited grand narrative about romantic love that's repeated in children's literature, television, film, and music. It's an unrealistic but intoxicating yardstick by which to measure our own relationships, even if unconsciously. The advertising industry and other forms of media culture have also placed a premium on unattainable perfection, which leaves many feeling they simply are not enough. It's not surprising that we settle not only in relationships with others, but also in our relationship with ourselves. The most toxic relationship a person has may be with him- or herself. We may berate, diminish, or judge ourselves. Or, we may try to change ourselves to fit what we perceive others want so that they will respond positively to us. We try to become what we think they want and we lose ourselves in the process.

I decided to write a novel about low-fat love so I could share what I had learned in an uncensored, honest way, with the hope and possibility that the kinds of women who had inspired me would read the book. Academic articles are often dry and rarely reach the public, so I wanted to use a more engaging and accessible form. I was hoping to push readers to reflect on their own lives, including their own roles in creating any dissatisfaction they experienced.

Low-Fat Love explores the psychology of negative relationships, identity building, and the social construction of femininity within popular culture, including how, too often, women become trapped in limited versions of themselves. Women's media is used as a signpost throughout the book in order to make visible the context in which women come to think of themselves, as well as the men and other women in their lives. Ultimately, the book explores women's identity struggles in relation to the men in their lives, and how women often develop myopic images of themselves as a part of "face-saving" strategies employed to cover up shame and a learned devaluation of self. *Low-Fat Love* encourages women to seek new ways to see that are not dependent on male approval so that they will value themselves and reject degrading relationships. Moreover, as the main characters in the book learn, a woman's relationship with herself may be her most toxic relationship. So, too, the men in *Low-Fat Love* learn that one must find one's voice or suffer the consequences. The novel is underscored with a message about self-acceptance.

Prilly Greene, the protagonist, spends most of her time tripping over her own insecurities as she attempts to negotiate a rollercoaster romance with a guy who can't give her what she really wants. His unconventional, free-spirited views on relationships unsettle her, ultimately causing her to unravel over the course of their on-again, off-again love affair. Meanwhile, Janice Goldwyn, a workaholic, feminist-in-name-only editor overburdens and belittles Prilly, her underling, with busywork and undercuts Prilly's professional identity. Prilly numbs herself with media aimed at women, causing her to feel worse about herself as she compares herself to celebrities and characters in made-for-television movies. Prilly longs for a "big life." Her emotional center rests on the belief that she is "in the middle"—not ugly or beautiful—and as a result, close enough to reach for the "big life" but perhaps never to attain it. Prilly lives in between who she is and who she longs to be. Ultimately, Prilly and Janice are each pushed to confront their images of themselves, exploring their insecurities, their attraction to men who withhold support, and their reasons for having settled for low-fat love.

Prilly hit a nerve with readers. I was bombarded with emails and routinely stopped in hallways after book talks or conference presentations by young women who saw bits of themselves in Prilly, even when they wished they hadn't. Strangers would whisper their stories of low-fat love to me. Some shared stories of divorce, domestic violence, sexual assault, eating disorders, alcoholism, dysfunctional relationships, heartbreak, grief, depression, and attempted suicide. I think the novel tapped into the loneliness many feel as they struggle with different versions of low-fat love. It wasn't just women, either; men were as enthusiastic and often wanted to talk with me about their girlfriends, sisters, daughters or themselves. In 2015 I released an expanded anniversary edition of *Low-Fat Love*, and new audiences found Prilly and the other characters. I still regularly receive emails from readers. I could never have anticipated the way the novel struck a chord. I don't have the words to express how grateful I am to all those who have taken the time to share their stories with me. I don't take it lightly.

As readers shared their stories with me, I learned more about low-fat love. I wanted to honor this new learning. It was these informal conversations and emails that prompted me to conduct a new set of interviews, this time seeking women across the age spectrum and explicitly seeking women who had experienced dissatisfying relationships, perhaps even with themselves. It is those interviews that are the basis of this book.

The stories my interviewees shared were raw, layered, and deeply emotional. I had visceral reactions reading them, and was moved to tears many times. My goal was to honor the texture and tone of what each woman shared. I invited creative arts therapist and visual artist Victoria Scotti to collaborate. Together we embarked on this joint project with the purpose of honestly transmitting the women's stories in a way that would allow readers their own visceral, emotional, and intellectual reactions. We created the "textual-visual snapshots" that comprise this book. Our hope is that these snapshots prompt self- and social reflection so that we each engage in a critical examination of our own lives, learn to value ourselves, and reject the grand cultural narratives that tell us we are never enough.

Patricia Leavy

ACKNOWLEDGEMENTS

In the work towards this book there are many to whom we are indebted. First and foremost, we extend our deepest gratitude to the remarkable women who bravely shared their stories with us. We are grateful for your candor, wisdom and honesty. We know that others will see themselves in your stories, and they will be better for it. This book is for you.

We are also enormously appreciative to Sense Publishers. Thank you Peter de Liefde, publisher extraordinaire, for your unfailing support of creativity. Thank you to the entire team at Sense Publishers, particularly Paul Chambers for your tireless marketing efforts, Jolanda Karada for your outstanding production assistance, and Robert van Gameren and Edwin Bakker for your assistance getting copies out.

We are proud to work with Clear Voice Editing. Thank you for your outstanding copy editing services. We are also grateful to Patricia's assistant, Shalen Lowell. Thank you for your help with the literature review and many other details. We also extend our appreciation to the editorial advisory board members of the *Social Fictions* series, and to the early reviewers for your generous endorsements. Thank you to our colleague, Dr. Sandra Faulkner, for your invaluable feedback. Finally, thank you Dr. Nancy Gerber for facilitating this collaborative project.

PATRICIA'S PERSONAL ACKNOWLEDGEMENTS

My deep gratitude to my colleagues, friends, and family, especially Ally Field, Monique Robitaille, Melissa Anyiwo, Pamela DeSantis, Laurel Richardson, Tori Amos, Adrienne Trier-Bieniek, Jessica Smartt Gullion, Sandra Faulkner, Anne Harris, Mr. Barry Mark Shuman, and Vanessa Alssid. Special thanks to Celine Boyle for your feedback and friendship along the way. Madeline Leavy-Rosen, I love you more than all the stars in the sky. I hope you never settle for low-fat love because you deserve the real deal. Always bet on yourself. Mark Robins, thanks for filling my life with the real thing. Much love.

VICTORIA'S PERSONAL ACKNOWLEDGEMENTS

First and foremost, I would like to express my great appreciation to Dr. Nancy Gerber. Thank you for believing in me. Your passion for arts-based research and dedication to creativity and innovation guided me throughout this project. I would also like to thank my colleagues and friends, and especially Dr. Gioia Chilton for her support. A heartfelt thank you to my husband, Anthony Scotti, and our children Isabella and Tonio for your enduring love and patience.

INTRODUCTION

Low-Fat Love Stories is a collection of sixteen short stories and visual portraits based directly on interview research with women about a dissatisfying relationship, either with a romantic partner or family member, or their body image. "Dissatisfying" was not defined for the women, allowing each to interpret the term in her own way. The stories focus on settling in relationships, toxic dynamics, the gap between fantasies and realities, recognizing and breaking relationship patterns, feeling like a fraud, divorce, abuse, spirituality, confronting childhood pain, daily struggles facing the mirror, growing older, and more. Language was taken directly from each woman's interview transcript to construct her story. We kept their first-person narration to bring you into the minds and experiences of the women.

Moreover, this book features visual art that is inseparable from the stories. Portraiture conveys the women's experiences. Portraits are often thought to depict the physical aspects of a person, but they can also convey emotions, states of mind, past experiences, and hopes and fantasies (Brilliant, 2002; Freeland, 2010; West, 2004). As human beings, we relate to each other through our expression of emotions. In this book, the women's expressions, as well as the details that are depicted in the portraits, invite you to reflect on their experiences, your own, and perhaps will foster empathy across similarities and differences.

The format of the "textual-visual snapshots," as we call them, is an emergent arts-based research practice we have developed. We invite you to follow our process of creating the stories and the art. When we present our work at conferences, audience members often wonder about the process of creating social fiction (Leavy, 2011, 2015) and representations in arts-based research. In this book, we make this process visible. Each woman's experience is contextualized within some basic information about her: age, ethnicity, sexuality, etc. This is followed by an initial portrait sketch; we termed this our "visual concept" that Victoria created directly based on the interview and demographic data. Following that, we present the story that Patricia created based on the draft portrait and interview transcript. Each woman's story concludes with the final portrait that Victoria reworked from the sketch, based on the story. By following the exchanges between different art forms, we hope that you will experience the process of their creation and feel the stories as you read and see them.

As a collection, the stories and art set you on an emotional rollercoaster. They are concomitantly raw, sad, visceral, challenging, inspirational, and hopeful. Together, the stories and art illustrate the many different forms low-fat love may take, as women search for ways to reject unhealthy relationships and value themselves. We hope these "textual-visual snapshots" inspire others to reject low-fat love in their own lives.

The thread throughout this book centers on issues of self-esteem and learning self-love. As many of the women represented in this book have learned, it is difficult or perhaps impossible to love others well until we learn to love ourselves. Yet this may be the most challenging kind of love to cultivate. Famed scholar bell hooks (2000) wrote a book titled *All About Love: New Visions*, consisting of thirteen chapters on different kinds of love. It's noteworthy that she said the chapter on self-love was the most difficult to write. In that chapter, hooks observes that self-love requires us not only to learn how we developed "feelings of worthlessness," but to engage in constructive behaviors to affirm our worth (2000, pp. 54–55). hooks further urges that cultivating self-love requires taking responsibility for our choices and developing an authentic self as opposed to a "false self, invented to please others," which will only lead to "fragile self-esteem" (2000, pp. 55–60). These sentiments come to life in the stories of the women represented in this book. The struggle to create self-love and an authentic identity from which we can draw positive esteem is arguably made more difficult when we are socialized in environments that minimize and stereotype women.

POPULAR CULTURE

Popular culture refers to the images, narratives, and ideas that circulate within mainstream or media culture (Leavy & Trier-Bieniek, 2014, p. 12). Media culture is a major agent of socialization through which we learn the norms and values of the society in which we live (Leavy & Trier-Bieniek, 2014, p. 13). With respect to the topics covered in this book, popular culture informs our ideas about romantic relationships, sex, family, femininity, masculinity, and what is attractive, among other things. We must consider who is producing popular media and what the content portrays.

While there is no doubt that men can suffer from low-fat love, we chose to focus on women, to give voice to women's unique and often untold stories. The context in which men and women develop a sense of self is itself highly gendered in ways that impact women's experiences, because our identities don't develop in a vacuum (Jhally, 1990). Popular culture is a significant part of the context in which people in the United States and many other parts of the Western world develop a sense of self. For example, Americans are bombarded with thousands of advertisements each day. If you go online, watch television or movies, read the news or magazines, or even see billboards as you drive down the highway, you are exposed. Renowned media scholar Jean Kilbourne (1999, 2010) notes that nearly everyone feels personally exempt from the impact of advertising, but they aren't.

Popular culture is predominantly created by men and thus reflects male ways of looking at the world. Here are some stats from the film industry in 2015 (Lauzen, 2016):

- Men were 91% of directors.
- Men were 89% of writers.
- Men were 74% of producers.
- Men were 80% of executive producers.
- Men were 78% of editors.
- Men were 94% of cinematographers.

Television didn't fare much better. Here are some stats from 2014/2015 (Lauzen, 2015):

- Men were 73% of creators, directors, writers, producers, executive producers, editors, and directors of photography working on broadcast programs.
- Men were 75% of those in the same roles on broadcast, cable and Netflix programs.

The advertising industry also shows enormous gender disparity. In 2015, men were 89% of creative directors (Hanan, 2016).

Although the disparity is not as extreme, news reporting has not been immune from this gender inequality. Here are some stats for news reporting in 2014 (Women's Media Center, 2015):

- Men reported 65% of all U. S. political news stories.
- Men generated 62.1% of news overall.
- Men wrote 62% of all print news stories in 10 of the most widely circulated newspapers.
- Men wrote 58% of Internet news content at four online news sites.
- Men were on camera in evening broadcast news 68% of the time. These include appearances by anchors as well as correspondents.

Overall, the production of the media landscape is male-dominated. How does this impact the content? What kinds of stories and portrayals come out of this media world? How might they impact how women feel about themselves and envision relationships?

Popular culture overwhelmingly presents women as relational, with personal relationships taking primacy in their lives, much more so than for men. For example, consider the kinds of roles male and female characters are shown in. Here are some stats for television and film roles in 2014 (Cipriani, 2015):

- Male characters were more likely than females to be identified only by a work-related role, such as doctor or business executive (61% of males vs. 34% of females).
- Female characters were more likely than males to be identified only by a personal life-related role such as wife or mother (58% of females vs. 31% of males).

- Male characters were more likely than females to have an identifiable goal (60% vs. 49%).
- Male characters were more likely than female characters to have work-related goals (48% vs. 34%) or crime-related goals (7% vs. 2%).
- Female characters were more likely than males to have goals related to their personal lives (14% vs. 5%).

It's important to remember that most of us are exposed to the narratives in popular culture from a young age. Consider, for example, the content of most fairytales. While today there are alternatives such as *Shrek, Maleficent,* and *Frozen,* the women interviewed for this book were likely exposed to *Cinderella, Snow White, Sleeping Beauty, The Little Mermaid, Beauty and the Beast,* and *Aladdin.* These stories present very traditional and limited versions of gender roles, femininity sexuality, and youth, and often emphasize the primacy of romantic love at all costs for women. Many of these stories also pit women against each other. Our interviews echo these themes.

This is all part of the context in which the women interviewed have developed their senses of self, including their ideas about relationships (what they should look like, feel like, and how important they are). We suggest this is a part of the context for understanding women's experiences with low-fat love.

Bear in mind that popular culture and media are highly visual. The portrayal of women in popular media has been the subject of ongoing analysis by scholars, artists, and media critics for decades (Breines, Crocker, & Garcia, 2008; Chrisler, 2011; Harris, 2003; Paquette & Raine, 2004; Scott & Derry, 2005; Wolszon, 1998). To present a response to popular culture, or as an act of resistance, this book also features representations of women, but they are different from those often portrayed in popular culture. For example, some of the stories and portraits in this book emphasize the discrepancy between how a particular woman really feels and how she tries to appear in order to fit into the framework portrayed in the culture. In these instances, women feel helpless, anxious, fraudulent, and ultimately unhappy. To reveal these emotional states, the portraits featured in this book are not representations of how the women look, but rather how they feel. We consider the portrayal of feelings in their own bodies to more fully realize the real representation of women's experiences.

THE INTERVIEWS AND METHOD

Fifty-six women ranging in age from their twenties to seventies were interviewed for this book, with approximately half being in their fifties. Women were recruited online, and interviews were conducted via email so that women from all over the United States could participate. By conducting the interviews in this format the women were also given time and space to reflect on their experiences and write them down in their own language. In the spirit of Eve Ensler's work (for example, the 1996 play *The Vagina Monologues*), we asked women to talk about that which is often rendered invisible. Women could focus their interviews on a dissatisfying relationship with a romantic partner, family member, friend or colleague, or they could focus on body image and identity. All the women elected to focus on a relationship with a romantic partner, family member, or their body image. All the interviews were coded and analyzed, and ultimately seventeen women's interviews were selected, which are represented in sixteen stories and portraits. The stories are representative of all of the themes that emerged from the interview data, including love, settling, regret, grief, childhood abuse, violence, financial abuse, marriage, divorce, break-ups, companionship, relationship conventions, sexual problems, dysfunctional relationship patterns and patterns of communication, rebuilding oneself, professional identity, family discord, mother-daughter relationships, sibling rivalry, feeling like a fraud, aging, spirituality, body image dissatisfaction (thinness aspirations, dental concerns, wrinkles, and unhappiness with breasts were frequently recurring themes), eating and exercise habits, popular culture consumption, and body image satisfaction. We also accounted for a range of sexualities, race, religion and ages. While only seventeen women's interview transcripts were directly used, what we learned from all the women informs the stories in this book.

The method we developed for this project involved a back and forth between written text and visual art that resulted in "textual-visual snapshots." We decided to bridge the genres of short story and visual art for two reasons. First, by iteratively responding to the data using different art forms, we came to a more intimate understanding of the participant's experience. Second, that relationality allowed us to represent the participant's experience more fully in written and visual forms. The iterative process included the following steps. After categorizing and analyzing the interview data, Patricia typed summaries of the seventeen interviews, ranging from two to three single-spaced pages. The summaries included demographic information, key themes to emerge in the interview, and the standout direct quotes from the interview. Victoria then used the summaries to create a "visual concept" for the woman. We consider this another act of analysis. She used portraiture, which allowed her to focus on the woman, her emotions, and experiences. The visual concept was intended to capture the themes and tone of the interview. Patricia then used the visual concept for inspiration in writing each story. The stories comprise verbatim transcript text along with Patricia's own words, woven together to shape a short narrative. Overall, the stories rely on roughly fifty percent direct language from the interviews, although there is variation across the book. The goal was to best tell each woman's story, communicating the essence of her experience, while maintaining her precise language when possible.

Patricia then sent Victoria each woman's story, and Victoria created the woman's final portrait in response to the story. The purpose of the final portrait was to create a concise and visceral representation of the participant's experience. Images are not linear; they have the capacity to carry multiple meanings simultaneously. These portraits connect the past and the present, the objective reality and the fantasy, and illustrate the participant's relationships. The portraits are not intended in any way to represent what these women actually look like (we have no idea what they look like), but rather, they represent the themes and texture of the interview. The portraits represent the stories, and the stories represent the portraits: they are inseparable. While each story and portrait is unique to one woman's particular experience, they also carry the experiences of many. While we call the combination of words and images "snapshots," they are multilayered, referencing experiences a woman may have had over her lifetime.

We gave each woman a pseudonym, and liberties were taken in fictionalizing aspects of their stories. For a more detailed discussion of our method, including the artistic techniques employed, please see Appendix A.

READING THIS BOOK

These stories can be read one or two at a time, or all in one sitting. While the stories are quite short, they are intended to be powerful punches that solicit reflection. Likewise, the art can be meditated upon and revisited in order to "see" more. They are layered. While the stories have been curated, they can also be read out of order.

This book can be used as supplemental reading in a range of college courses that deal with gender, family, relational communication, psychology, sociology, and social work. It can also be used as an exemplar in courses on qualitative inquiry, arts-based research, narrative inquiry, or creative writing. Finally, this book can be read entirely for pleasure by individual readers or book clubs. The section titled "Further Engagement" at the end of the book includes discussion or thought questions, as well as creative writing, qualitative research, arts-based research, and artistic activities. These can be used in classes as well as by individual readers looking for different ways to reflect on the stories and their own lives.

REFERENCES

Breines, J. G., Crocker, J., & Garcia, J. A. (2008). Self-objectification and well-being in women's daily lives. *Personality Social Psychology Bulletin, 34*, 583–598. doi:10.1177/0146167207313727

Brilliant, R. (2002). *Portraiture*. London, UK: Reaktion Books.

Chrisler, J. (2011). Feminist psychology and the ''Body Problem'': Sexuality, physical appearance, and women's physical and mental health. *Psychology of Women Quarterly, 34*(4), 648–654. doi:10.1177/0361684311426688

Cipriani, C. (2015, February 10). Sorry, ladies: Study on women in film and television confirms the worst. *Indiewire*. Retrieved from http://www.indiewire.com/2015/02/sorry-ladies-study-on-women-in-film-and-television-confirms-the-worst-65220/

Freeland, C. (2010). *Portraits and persons: A philosophical inquiry*. New York, NY: Oxford University Press.

Hanan, A. (2016, February 3). Five facts that show how the advertising industry fails women. *The Guardian*. Retrieved from https://www.theguardian.com/women-in-leadership/2016/feb/03/how-advertising-industry-fails-women

Harris, V. (2003). Images of women's health and healing: Cultural prescriptions? In F. Poland & G. Boswell (Eds.), *Women's minds, women's bodies: An interdisciplinary approach to women's health* (pp. 21–35).Basingstoke, UK: Palgrave Macmillan.

hooks, b. (2000). *All about love: New visions*. New York, NY: Harper Perennial.

Jhally, S. (1990). *The codes of advertising: Fetishism and the political economy of meaning in the consumer society*. New York, NY: Routledge.

Kilbourne, J. (1999). *Deadly persuasion: Why women and girls must fight the addictive power of advertising*. New York, NY: The Free Press.

Kilbourne, J. (Creator), & Jhally, S. (Director). (2010). *Killing us softly 4: Advertising's image of women* [Motion picture]. US: Media Education Foundation.

Lauzen, M. M. (2015). *Boxed in: Portrayals of female characters and employment of behind-the-scenes women in 2014–15 prime-time television*. Retrieved from http://womenintvfilm.sdsu.edu/files/2014-15_Boxed_In_Report.pdf

Lauzen, M. M. (2016). *The celluloid ceiling: Behind-the-scenes employment of women on the top 100, 250, and 500 films of 2015*. Retrieved from http://womenintvfilm.sdsu.edu/files/2015_Celluloid_Ceiling_Report.pdf

Leavy, P. (2011). *Low-fat love*. Rotterdam, The Netherlands: Sense Publishers.

Leavy, P. (2015). *Low-fat love: Expanded anniversary edition*. Rotterdam, The Netherlands: Sense Publishers.

Leavy, P. (2015). *Method meets art: Arts-based research practice*. New York, NY: Guilford Press.

Leavy, P., & Trier-Bieniek, A. (2014). Introduction to gender & pop culture. In A. Trier-Bieniek & P. Leavy (Eds.), *Gender & pop culture: A text-reader* (pp. 1–25). Rotterdam, The Netherlands: Sense Publishers.

Paquette, M.-C., & Raine, K. (2004). Sociocultural context of women's body image. *Social Science & Medicine, 59*, 1047–1058.

Scott, B. A., & Derry, J. A. (2005). Women in their bodies: Challenging objectification through experiential learning. *Women's Studies Quarterly, 33*(1/2), 188–209.

The Vagina Monologues. By Eve Ensler. HERE Arts Center, New York City, October-November, 1996. Performance.

West, S. (2004). *Portraiture* (Oxford History of Art). New York, NY: Oxford University Press. Kindle Edition.

Wolszon, L. (1998). Women's body image theory and research. *The American Behavioral Scientist, 41*(4), 542–557.

Women's Media Center. (2015). *WMC divided 2015: The media gender gap*. Retrieved from http://www.womensmediacenter.com/pages/2015-wmc-divided-media-gender-gap

LEALA

59 years old
Sexual orientation not given
Latina
Religion not given

I put my life in his hands. He validated me, he gave me a sense of self-worth from the outside because I did not have it coming from the inside. This relationship was my entire world.

He hijacked my house, he destroyed our relationship, he sabotaged my retirement.

My relationship was out of balance because I gave my fiancée the power to control me, to validate me, to make me feel worthwhile.

Leala

CHAPTER 2

LIGHT MY OWN FIRE

Once upon a time, I met the man of my dreams. We were in a ballroom dancing class. Like a fairytale, I twirled right into his arms. Maybe that's not exactly how it happened, but it's how I remember it. He was tall, dark, handsome, and successful. He was well-respected. And sexy. So damn sexy. I looked up to him. He was the most charismatic person I had ever met. Everyone was enamored by his charm; some people ooze something that makes you want to be near them. He was like that. He was highly skilled in making you feel that you were the only person in the room, the only person who mattered. I never met anyone like that before, and I was totally captivated by him. I couldn't believe that someone like him wanted me. Each time he glanced my way with his sly smile, I melted. From the very beginning, I always thought he was too good for me.

I knew he had baggage. He was divorced, with adult children and financial messiness. I was willing to overlook it all. None of that mattered. I'd found a wonderful man. I wished I could spend all of my time with him. Due to the demands and location of my job, we lived a distance from each other but spent every other weekend together for many years. We danced, we played golf, we played tennis; we loved going to the theater, kayaking, and just being together. We always wanted to do things with each other. My life expanded. I truly loved him and believed that he loved me. For many years I was blissfully happy.

Everyone thought that we were the perfect couple. I thought so, too. It seemed perfect.

I never thought about my life outside of him, or us. This relationship was my entire world. I had no friends and no family to speak of. He was the center of my life. I worked an extremely demanding job, long hours, with a lot of travel. It was exhausting and didn't leave time for anything other than him, so I didn't spend a lot of time or effort looking outside the relationship for entertainment, companionship, or comfort. He was my entire world, and my identity was attributed to him. I didn't exist outside of my job and my relationship. I was happy and didn't see what a perilous situation I'd put myself in. Only now, looking back, do I realize how much I relied upon him and how much of myself I'd handed over to him. When a relationship is all-consuming, it's easy to get lost in it—to want to get lost in it. I had found my real-life Prince Charming. As far as I was concerned, or anyone else looking from the outside was concerned, I had everything. The moment he proposed was the happiest of my life.

He outstretched his hand, revealing a small, velvet box. He opened the box and a brilliant diamond sparkled at me.

"Will you marry me?" he asked in his sexiest voice.

I can't believe this is really happening. He actually wants me, I thought before emphatically saying, "Yes!" I was so overjoyed I shook with excitement. I was head over heels in love with this man.

After we became engaged, everything started to unravel. Fairytales have an underside, a shadow side. My castle was about to crumble. My prince would burn it down, and with it, the entire fairytale illusion. He was a dark prince.

I knew he had toxic finances. He owed money on college loans for his kids, the divorce settlement to his former wife, and a buyout provision to his business partner. I ignored it all. When he was looking for a place to live, I rented him my investment house. It made perfect sense. One day that house would fund my retirement, which we would spend together. That house represented our chance at happily ever after. It would be our version of riding off into the sunset. He paid me a meager rent, enough to cover basic expenses. I lived in a small condo close to my job and the airport. I visited him at the house every other weekend.

Once we decided to get married, he started to change. It was so subtle at first that I thought I might be imagining it. He would offer an unkind word or grunt in response to something I said. The impetus was usually if I made a remark about wanting to retire and sell the house. Soon his slights were no longer ambiguous. Somewhere along the line he became very greedy and then very belligerent. Instead of being excited at the prospect that we'd have more time together if I retired, he tried to convince me to keep working. He became overbearing. It was as if he thought he could control me, my thoughts, my desires, and my money. I repeatedly posed vehement objections to his attempt to control my financial life. The house was no longer a dream for the future, but rather a thing for him to possess, just like I had become.

Exhausted from years of hard work and commuting, I wanted to downsize, enabling us to spend our married years together. I wanted more than four days a month together. When I became determined to retire and sell my house, our relationship fell apart. All he cared about was staying in my house, which I couldn't afford unless I kept working. He told everyone in the community I was trying to uproot him and end his happiness. No one knew the house belonged only to me. He lied. The man who had always listened to me in the past began to ridicule me. He would not listen to me or accept my point of view. He bullied and badgered me. He sneered at me. He mocked me. He criticized me publicly. Without his validation, I fell into a deep hole. How could I live in a world where fairytales don't come true?

Because I had been happy before our engagement and his attempt to take financial control over my life, I wondered if the act of becoming engaged had changed him. Maybe he really didn't want to marry me and this was his way of destroying the relationship. Was it my fault? Eventually I came to understand that he had lied about many things over the course of our relationship. He changed stories, exaggerated details, and simply made things up. He had created an imaginary life and persona for our neighbors. He was a professional liar. By the end, when we went out he had to brief me on what he had told other people. I knew deep in my heart that the relationship was completely over. I thought I was going to die.

Being brought to my knees was humbling. I knew I was at a crossroads. I decided to save myself. First, I had to confront a dark truth. I had handed over my complete self-image, my complete self-worth. I put my life in his hands. He validated me and gave me a sense of self-worth from the outside because I did not have it coming from the inside. I needed to accept responsibility for my own self-worth. No one can hijack your life unless you allow them to.

I had to recognize that I have value with or without a man. My value comes from inside, who I am, not from the outside. I needed to accept full responsibility for my own happiness, for my own self-

LEALA

image, and for my own worth. No one has to take care of me, no one can complete me, no one is needed to make me a whole person.

I was attracted to his charismatic energy because I didn't think I had any of my own. I tried to draw strength from him like a parasite, and that's how he treated me. And I was comfortable that way. It took me a long time to realize that I wasn't looking up to him, but rather he was looking down on me. A dark, foreboding force, casting his shadow over me. I was curled up in a ball, at his feet, tied and bound willingly by my own choices. By my own choices.

I didn't need to draw energy from a charming man. I needed to learn to tap into my own energy. With renewed focus, I became a creative force. I became the architect of my own life. When I eventually did retire, I searched within for my own worth and passion. I took what I had learned about finding an authentic sense of self and I wrote a book, blogged, and shared my story on radio shows. I was able to recover from these catastrophic events in my life and then go on to teach others how to do the same. This was empowering. I built an identity that wasn't dependent on anyone else. I took the sullied fairytale, the dying embers from our crumbled castle, and used them to light my own fire.

ADDISON

60 years old
Sexual orientation not given
Race not given
Religion not given

My mother made me feel that
her life depended on me Or maybe
I just felt that way. At any rate,
I was called on to "save" her
multiple times and I felt I had to.

After years of declaring I was
nothing like my mom,
I see that I am ... I had to
work through a lot of feelings
and forgiveness...

Addison

DUALITY

March 20

"Your stepfather called again."

"He's unbelievable. He's not my stepfather anymore. Call him Stanley. God, they divorced decades ago."

"He wants to make sure you don't leave anything valuable behind when you pack up your mother's stuff. He says she promised him a watch and some other things."

"He's really something. The only things of value she had are gifts I gave her. He's such a narcissist."

"You know how I feel about your family, but at this point why get upset?"

"The focus on money and material things has haunted me my whole life. When my father died and split his estate between me and my mom, it made my mother and sisters resentful of me. Notwithstanding the fact that they're all batshit crazy, I know it was the end of any chance of a relationship with any of them. I was only two! Even though we all learned years later that this was a typical tax maneuver in the 1950s, it did nothing to dissuade the resentment that had built up."

"I know, honey. You've told me all of this."

"Well, it all got much worse when my mother married Stanley. He tried to cause rifts and he was so demeaning. He talked all the time about my 'lucky bucks' and both my sisters resented and hated me for this. Did I tell you what he did when I turned 21? He summoned me to his office and borrowed a bunch of money from me, promising to pay interest, which he never did. My mother made him secure the loan to a piece of property and after that I was bound to his financial craziness."

"Look, you spent most of your adult life not dealing with these people at all, and after you clean out your mom's room tomorrow you'll be entirely done. Pack it all up and have someone drop it off at his house. Wash your hands of it."

I nodded and excused myself to go sit on the porch and read, but I couldn't focus on the page in front of me. I was consumed with thoughts of the past. Years of pain, madness, and dysfunction. My mother was a sick woman. When my father died he left me an emotional invalid to take care of. I was just a child. No one raised in a normal family could ever understand. She must have been bipolar, but that's not something we knew about. I never knew what reaction I'd get from her.

She made me feel that her life depended on me. Maybe I just felt that way. I'll never know if she really wanted to hurt herself all those times, or if she yearned for attention, or worse, wanted to hurt me. I was called on to save her multiple times, and felt I had to. I'll never forget the night I spent talking her out of suicide. I was a teenager. The fear, thinking your mother may end herself if you can't save her is entirely overwhelming. The internal questions are relentless: *How could she hate herself when I love her? How could she abandon me? Why isn't my family normal? What if people find out? Can I love her enough? Can I always be there to protect her?*

Ten years later I had to arrange for her to be institutionalized because of another suicide threat. There were many other times she depended on me. The years we didn't speak at all offered a respite. I lost my best friend, but I gained my freedom. I could breathe. I could be. I could become someone outside of the cycle of craziness. There's no way anyone can really understand what it was like, all of those years, being held captive by her desperation to be saved.

What hurt me the most was how badly she'd treat me anytime I showed the slightest sign of creating an identity for myself. An identity not based on her. As I grew up I thought she was my best friend, but she hated me for every step I made to individuate myself. She had no boundaries.

The difficulty began in her own childhood. Her mother made her feel unloved. She confessed to me that her mother once told her, "I can't believe I hated you as a child." I think she suffered that most of her life and never really learned how to love.

March 21

I miss my mom. Cleaning out her room today, in the residential facility she lived in for the last years of her life, was one last thing I, the person she seemed to hate, or maybe the one person she loved the most, could do for her. Before Alzheimer's I would have said hate, but my mother and I had two relationships. The one after Alzheimer's was beautiful.

I can't believe how incredibly sad I felt sifting through her drawers of pictures, papers, and trinkets. I wasn't thinking about Stanley, my sisters, or my screwed-up childhood. I thought about the complicated, and in some ways remarkable, woman my mother was. The last three years were healing, even more than I had realized. The years of screaming matches, periods of not talking, and my own desperation to untie myself from her all seemed to fade away and make a space for something new. After Alzheimer's, things were different.

At first her Alzheimer's looked much like her insanity. Of her three children, she chose me to blame for everything, from leaving her in a geriatric psych ward to stealing her money. My guess is that this is because she felt safest with me.

Later, when she descended fully into Alzheimer's, I saw her three times a week and our visits were always sweet, filled with love. At first I couldn't believe how she'd light up when I walked into the room. Every time. We'd stroll, singing and holding hands. The staff even called us "the twins." She told me I was beautiful too many times to count. She stroked my face. We were incredibly tender with each other.

In the years before, our conversations were all over the place. They could be cold or loving. I believe most were honest, which is something I have come to value. After her Alzheimer's, they were all sweet. It was such a difficult relationship for so many years, and to have it end sweetly was amazing. I can honestly say I miss her so much now.

I guess I don't know who I would be without having had this relationship. She defined me for many years and loved me so much at the end. Finally, after years of declaring I was nothing like my mom, I see that I am: her kindness and caring for others, her compassion, her eyes. We're all responding in life to an audio recording playing over and over again in our minds. The words and phrases that stick in our minds and continue to damage or inspire us. The voices we hear until we find our own voices. Somewhere during her illness, the narrative in my head switched from *Don't let me become you,* to I *have become the best of you.*

I also feel that much of my life was in opposition to her. Now I find myself mourning the sweet woman who lived with Alzheimer's. I had to work through a lot of feelings and forgiveness before I could once again take responsibility for her as she entered dementia. But our last years together were very openhearted.

People think that Alzheimer's steals their loved ones, and that is true for many. I was lucky. For my mother and me, it was the opposite. There can be a very deep love that's covered up with lots of crap, and when the crap leaves you're left with the glory of the true affections. Ironically, the best relationship we had was between me, her, and her Alzheimer's. The sweet relationship of Alzheimer's removed the resentments and hatreds. In the end, I held her and caressed her head, finally giving her what perhaps she always wanted, but didn't know how to get: unconditional love.

CHAPTER 4

VALERIE

53 years old
Sexual orientation not given
Race not given
Religion not given

THE EMOTIONAL CONTORTIONIST

The whirlwind of feelings when Jesse died soon felt like a tornado, sweeping me up. They were overpowering and contradictory, mirroring our relationship. I was deeply saddened, relieved that he wasn't suffering, and frightened. I was also grateful. In his death I was given a socially acceptable way to let go of the challenges in our marriage. After 12 years, I was free. When the storm of emotions passed, I was still standing among the wreckage, determined to re-create my life.

Now that I am worlds away from the woman I was then, it's become clear that the beginning of our relationship contained the key and the trapdoor. I had been trying to figure out who I was. Desperate for a purpose, longing to feel whole, I turned to spirituality. I was walking a spiritual path and traveling with writers, teachers, and healers to find ways of being of service. A message from The Spirit convinced me to cancel a trip overseas and instead tag along with a group of friends to hear a beloved spiritual teacher speak, an hour away from my home. During the intermission a mutual friend introduced me to Jesse.

"A pleasure to meet you," he said as he offered his hand. His cobalt eyes and warm, engaging smile drew me in.

"Nice to meet you too," I said, as my hand touched his.

"The talk is powerful. Don't you think?" he asked.

"Yes. Very inspiring."

It's impossible to separate the space in which we met from the instant connection. We were two souls in search of meaning, beautifully desperate for personal and spiritual growth. We were high on hope.

The love was fast and hard. Within a few months we lived together, and seven months after meeting, we married. Our relationship was nurturing, passionate, and infinitely enticing.

"You are the best thing that ever happened to me," he would say. And then the words I could never hear enough: "You are the love of my life."

Onto that love I projected my vision of us as a spiritual power couple. The more I believed in that dream, the more its haunted underside, its nightmare side, revealed itself, challenging me to the core.

Jesse had a traumatizing childhood. The scars ran deep, imprisoning his mind and warping his innately nurturing heart. At times he allowed his childhood wounds and anger to run his life, and to impact mine. As a social worker and therapist, I now realize the scars that essentially tied me to a lie had begun as a source of attraction. I expected that the love I had to offer would heal his wounds so he could find peace. I wanted to save him. I thought that was my purpose.

I never knew when the wind would turn from a whisper to a roar. He could become controlling, arrogant, and emotionally abusive. If I didn't agree with him about something, he accused me of being disloyal. Loyalty was the constant test, the weapon. In difficult moments he couldn't accept the love I thought would heal him. His reactions to the slightest conflict or difference of opinion ranged from withdrawing, shutting down, name-calling, putdowns, to outright explosions. It was rare that we could talk things through calmly. We were tethered together in an obstacle course of old wounds. Landmines were everywhere.

For me, there was no greater burden than silence, but the truth would have decimated the façade that we were a spiritual power couple. The truth would have shattered my identity.

I felt hypocritical since I counseled other women about unhealthy relationship issues and encouraged them to find a way to change the dynamics or leave the relationship. I questioned myself as a social worker. My biggest fear played over and over in my mind: *How would it look if I were in a relationship that had elements of abuse in it?* I was terrified of being exposed as a fraud, so I kept it under wraps. When an explosion occurred, I scrambled to find solutions to keep the peace. I cried alone. If I spoke with friends, I minimized how challenging it was and I tried to explain away his behavior. Then, one night, things went too far.

I came home from work, tired from a long day. Jesse was on the phone. I could tell right away that he was talking to his brother. He always tensed up when he spoke with him. I headed straight into the kitchen to make dinner. I had prepared a chicken for roasting and had started peeling some carrots over the sink when Jesse hung up and came in the room. Without acknowledging my presence, he poured himself a bourbon. He threw it back while leaning over the kitchen counter. He then started rambling on about what a jerk his older brother was.

"Well, at least he's trying to make things better," I said, in an effort to focus on the positive.

Jesse was furious. He didn't deal well with anything he perceived as criticism, especially if I didn't take his side against his family. I was being disloyal, a traitor, an enemy. He yelled at me, and I yelled in return. Before I knew it, he picked up his empty glass and threw it in anger. I think he meant to hit the wall, but it hit me. Fortunately, the glass didn't break until it crashed on the floor, but in that moment any remaining hope I had for the couple I had imagined we were was shattered.

Mortified, tearful, and deeply apologetic, Jesse immediately ran to my side. "Oh my God, I'm so sorry. I'm so sorry. I can't believe I did that," he repeated over and over again.

As he knelt on the floor brushing the glass into a dustpan, crying hysterically, he mumbled, "I would understand if you want to leave me."

"I will stay," I said, "but this can never happen again."

I consoled him for hours before he cried himself to sleep. I lay awake all night. The next morning the kitchen reeked from the raw chicken left on the counter. I felt like I was staring at the carcass of the life I had dreamed up. I could no longer avoid looking at the man behind the screen. I couldn't cover the stench with perfume. But I was fearful of leaving, since so much of our lives were linked together. I was worried what people would think. So I stayed.

Jesse was true to his word and there was never any more physical violence. While we had many beautiful times, and I know he loved me deeply, we were never able to escape his wounds, my need to please, or the image we had created for the gaze of others. That image cast a shadow over everything.

When I think back on it, we were actors performing the role of a spiritual power couple. We were trapped in a circus we had constructed. Dazzling costumes conceal the truth that many circus performers' dreams have not been realized. Their disappointments are masked by sequins and sleight-of-hand. Their failures are sugarcoated in cotton candy and caramel corn—sweet at first, but they rot your teeth until you're afraid to smile. Our life was like that. I can hear the ringmaster introducing me:

"And over here in the center ring, we have an emotional contortionist who will bend over backwards to please people, a deer caught in the headlights, always looking over her shoulder to see if the propriety police are watching."

I'd enter the ring, sparkling from head to toe, with a plastered smile on my face. With Jesse's death, this performer took her final bow.

JANE

28 years old
Heterosexual
Caucasian
Roman Catholic

PRETTY

You're naturally pretty.
If you're not skinny you can't be successful.
You can be thin, too, on our diet program.
No one wants to sleep with the fat girl, but she's good for a laugh.
You have skinny legs.
Thank you for losing weight.
I just want my thighs not to touch.
Pretty.
Skinny.
Thin.
Fat.
Thighs.
Pretty.
Skinny.
Thin.
Fat.
Thighs.

Ahhhhhhhhhh! The voices in my head: my father, my students, television, my friends. They're all in a loud rumble every time in look in the mirror. I can't get their voices out of my head. I'm tortured by them.

I hate the way I look. I hate myself like this. It's all I can think about, as if hating myself enough will make it better. When I looked in the mirror for the tenth time this morning I was horrified. My biggest problem is back fat. I especially noticed how bad it is when I turned around and peered back at the mirror. Awful. I can't stop looking at it, like looking in a refrigerator hoping a chocolate cake will suddenly appear. I keep hoping for my back fat to disappear. But it's not just back fat that I find disgusting, but my entire stomach, hip, and thigh area. It's gross. I'm gross.

It would be awesome if I was really skinny. I used to be skinny. Back then I always wished I could be skinnier. I thought that if I were skinnier it would all be better. Life would be better. Compared to how I am now, I guess I used to be skinny. Believe it or not, my dominant identity was as the hot girl. That's how people thought of me and it made me feel like I was someone. My appearance has always been one of the most important parts of me. Even though I was an honor student in high school and a great athlete, I always thought that if I didn't look the way I did, that I wouldn't have anything. That hasn't changed. Even now, having excelled in college and graduate school, and building a career as an academic, none of it matters. I just want my thighs not to touch.

During college and graduate school it all went to pot. My eating and exercise habits changed. I was under a lot of stress. Maybe it was age and my metabolism, too. I gained so much weight. I remember in my senior year of college my roommate and I decided to try the Weight Watchers points system. We wrote our weights on the fridge and I was 133 pounds. I remember thinking it would be so great if I could weigh 125 pounds. Looking back now, at 150 pounds, I would KILL to weigh 133. Throughout graduate school I gained about 20 pounds. This fall, I lost 10 pounds, but it's not nearly enough.

I look in the mirror and I feel disgusting, gross, and embarrassed. Sometimes I think the glass will shatter before my eyes, broken by my reflection. I go to great lengths to avoid letting people from high school see me; I'm fearful that they will see me and say, "Wow, she really let herself go," or "She really got fat after high school." They will wonder, "What happened to her?" I don't want any pictures taken of me and posted on Facebook for the same reason. I just want to stay in the house and not let anyone from my past see me. I even avoid my college friends. They always commented on my skinny limbs, so when those went away, it was like I had nothing left. I'm afraid of what people will say about me. I'm in a weird paradox, because my weight has made me feel like a spectacle and almost invisible at the same time. I have nothing to offer.

I hear myself say those words in my head, *I have nothing to offer*, and I'm embarrassed to call myself feminist. I'm petrified of being revealed. Today I expected to be caught being a fraud. I was showing Jean Kilbourne's film *Killing Us Softly 3* in my gender class and, as expected, the students had pretty strong reactions. Like usual, most of the women in class agreed that pop culture tells us that a woman's appearance is the most important thing about her and if you aren't as skinny as you can be, you won't be successful. There's only one way to be sexy and appealing to men, and that is to look like a Victoria's Secret model. If you're overweight, you cannot be sexy and any attempt at being sexy is laughable. Some students felt like debating and so they gave examples of celebrities who aren't super skinny and are still successful. But others chimed in and echoed what I was thinking, providing examples like Jessica Simpson, Mariah Carey, and Kirstie Alley and noting how they've been treated in the tabloids during the past few years as their weight has fluctuated. I was thinking about Melissa McCarthy's character from *Bridesmaids*. Whenever her character was trying to act sexy, it was for laughs. It really gets me when some students start talking about just tuning out the media, and then it won't impact them. As if it's that easy. There is essentially no way that women and girls can escape advertisements telling them that something about their appearance needs to be changed on a daily basis. Who are they kidding?

But I always worry about saying too much. I'm afraid they'll see how insecure I actually am. I'm already worried about how they perceive my appearance. I mean, it's obvious I care about fashion and trends. My style is very feminine and I wear makeup. Since I look young, I try to wear sophisticated clothes when I teach to make myself seem more legitimate, but I can't help worrying that it only draws attention to how hard I try to make myself look better than I actually do. My biggest fear is that in one of these class discussions I'll say something that shows them how profoundly impacted by the media I am. What would they think if they knew that I'm a pop culture junkie? I watch a lot of reality TV, have a subscription to *US Weekly*, and keep up with celebrity gossip daily on websites like Gawker, Jezebel, and Perez Hilton. I also love fashion magazines and know who the "it girl" models are. It's not that I don't know that pop culture is completely hypocritical in the ways it depicts women and their bodies. I know, and love it anyway. I'm terrified they'll find out. I mean, what kind of feminist am I? I feel like a fraud. My whole life seems to be a game of keeping up appearances in every respect. I'm afraid of being unmasked.

My father called tonight. His timing is impeccable. He asked how my diet was going. I mean, I told him it's a new workout routine, not a diet, but he never listens. He only cares about what I look like. He has always commented on my looks. Throughout my life, he would say that he wanted me to become Miss America and would address me by saying "Hi, Pretty." He would always tell me to wear my hair down, and not to wear makeup or nail polish because I'm "naturally beautiful." I always thought that the talk about "natural beauty" was sort of empowering. When he began making negative comments about my weight and appearance, I realized how damaging all of his comments about my appearance and body had been.

I was on the academic job market last year and whenever we had family gatherings or talked on the phone, he would ask how the process was going. Inevitably, he would add in, "Well remember, you have to get buff," meaning, lose weight. Then he began to add in interview tips like, "Make sure to show some cleavage," and "Dress sexy," because "he knows how men think." At first I tried to brush it off, telling myself that he doesn't know anything about academia and he's just trying to be helpful. Then he kept saying it over and over again, every time we would talk about jobs. Everything came to a head when we drove up to see my sister at school. He said something in the car and I totally blew up and told him I wasn't going to speak to him if he continued to make comments about my body. I didn't talk to him the rest of the trip but he just chalked it up to me "being bitchy" rather than reflecting on how his comments made me feel. I didn't talk to him for a few weeks and then we slowly began talking again. We never directly addressed why those comments had hurt me. I don't think it would have made a difference, anyway. He's been commenting on my mother's weight for 35 years.

Nothing will ever change with him. I mean, just yesterday I was home for a family dinner and at the end of the night, he came up to me, kissed me on the forehead and said, "Thank you for losing weight." I couldn't believe he thanked me for losing weight. Not, I am so proud of your teaching award last spring, or your recent publication. Thank you for losing weight. As if I did it for him. The really messed-up part was that I was glad my weight loss was noticeable. His comment kind of made me feel good. I was flattered. My hard work was paying off.

And in a weird way I did lose weight for him, for my boyfriend, for any random man walking down the street who might happen to notice me. I did it for them. And I keep doing it for them. I always think about how certain clothes or hairstyles will be perceived by men. Even though I want a new hairstyle, I am wary about cutting my hair since men like long hair. I'm an educated feminist obsessed with what men think about my looks. I can't help it.

Men want to be with a woman who looks like a celebrity, with a perfect body. My pop culture obsession is toxic. Beyoncé says, "Pretty hurts." But look at her. Seriously. What I remember from the video for that song is how beautiful she is. Ugly hurts more than pretty.

The truth I'm afraid to admit, that maybe other women are afraid to admit, is ugly. The deep, dark truth is I just want to be skinny, to be the hot girl again. If I were, I would be wanted by important men, people would envy me, and I would be powerful. I would be proud to be shown off as someone's girlfriend because I would be something rare: impossibly skinny, tall, and beautiful. No matter what was happening in the rest of my life, I would feel good since I would be happy with the way I looked. I wouldn't cry looking in the mirror. I wouldn't feel so torn apart. If only I were skinny.

Pretty.
Skinny.
Thin.
Fat.
I just want my thighs not to touch.

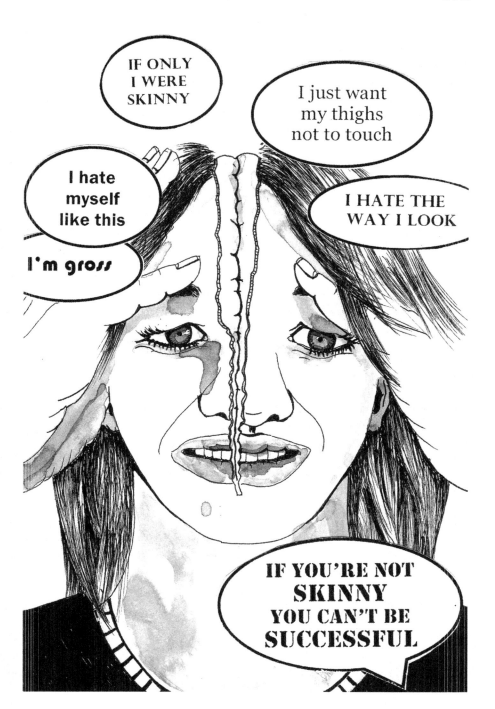

TIFFANY

26 years old
Heterosexual
Caucasian
Jewish

SEX DRIVE

"So over the phone you said you wanted to talk about your relationship. Tell me about your boyfriend, Jay. How did you meet?"

"We met by chance, online through a mutual friend. We had an AOL chat buddy in common and struck up a conversation one night. I was procrastinating doing work and was looking up a person with similar interests to chat with. We talked all night. After that, I found myself rushing home each day to get online to talk to him. After a few weeks we started talking on the phone. Then we met in person. We went on dates for weeks before we officially became a couple. It was very sweet and romantic."

"So you have a lot in common?"

"We are opposites overall, but it's never been an issue. He's incredibly witty and funny. I don't have a simple sense of humor, so if you can out-wit me, I melt a bit. He leaves me in tears from fits of laughter daily."

"How long have you been together?"

"Almost nine years. Exclusive. I'm very old-fashioned."

"Do you live together?"

"Yes. We moved in together six years ago, for about a year and a half and then I moved into my own place. I had never lived alone and we both thought it would be good for me, being so young. He's older. We wanted to make sure I wouldn't have any regrets later. I hated it, though. Loved my apartment but spent 90% of the time either at his place, or him at mine. When my 18-month lease was up, he asked me to move back in, which I did gladly. We still live together. It was a good experience, but I'm so glad it's over."

"Tell me about your relationship?"

"We are each other's best friends. He makes me very happy. I feel loved and respected. He brings out the best in me. I always want to do better and achieve more in life with him. We don't yell. We never really fight. We are usually very honest. We let each other have our own space and identities, but love to do most everything together. He's less social than I am, but I don't mind. No complaints."

"How important is this relationship to you?"

"He is my other half. Without him I wouldn't feel whole. Not to say I couldn't go on if something happened, but I wouldn't be the same person without him."

"You said you're exclusive. Have there been any fidelity concerns?"

"I personally had some issues to work out about trust. My parents had infidelity issues and I've always been a bit worried about being in a relationship where it happened. And so I would be overcautious and always try to search for signs to protect myself. And there were a few times I allowed my insecurities to get the best of me, but it was early on in the relationship."

"What happened at those times when you felt insecure?"

"The thing that brought that out—which I think is a very common dating issue—was the old 'I trust my boyfriend but I don't trust his female friends.' He had this one friend, Laura, and she's one of those very touchy, flirty kind of girls. They hung out a lot and I always felt like she was coming on to him. One weekend we had a big argument because he was going to a baseball game with her and I kind of freaked out. He was really offended that I didn't trust him. When I saw how stunned and hurt he was, I realized I had to be realistic about my issues. If I actually did trust him, then it canceled out the female friend who I may not trust or like. Because he wouldn't let it go anywhere if he was trustworthy. That's what I ended up realizing, which allowed me over time to be less worried about infidelity."

"So was there something specific on your mind that you wanted to talk about?"

"Um, there is but it's uh, it's sort of embarrassing."

"Take your time."

"I'm worried about our sex life. Neither of us feels sexually neglected, but . . . He had some health issues that don't allow him to perform as much as we used to. We went from three to four times a week, to weekly, and now we are about monthly. We don't have sex enough. Also, um . . ."

"Yes?"

"He wants more oral sex. I guess all guys do, right? I used to do it one to three times a week and now it's like a few times a year. I'm not a huge fan of doing it, mainly because with his age and medications, it takes longer for him to, you know. It makes me anxious to do it after a long day. Also, I'm not as inspired as I used to be. He used to be more sexually aggressive, but since his medical issues are cramping his sex drive it's left up to me to make all the moves. I work long days so I get tired, and once I get into bed, I want to sleep. Is this normal? Is this what happens in relationships over time?"

SHERRY

55 years old
Prefers male companionship
Caucasian
Spiritual not religious

DROWNING

Laura looked beautiful in her gown today. I can't believe my baby girl got married. And I still can't believe they picked Valentine's Day. You'd think having a mom on her third marriage would have tempered her feelings about romance. I'd like to think that she's influenced by the fact that I found a partner who is perfect, even if it is the third time around. Yet I have no doubt that a part of her still wishes I was with her dad, especially on big days. She knows we've tried to be nice to each other during events like her sweet 16 party, her graduation, and of course today. But it's still uncomfortable.

Standing just feet away from Burt, as our daughter promised to love someone forever, did make me think about our failed marriage. Sixteen years is quite a stretch. In the beginning, I was happy. I still don't know how the ending was such a far distance from the beginning.

There was a time when I was in love with Burt. There were the little things, like we both loved going to movies every weekend. I was so happy to have someone to do things with. My first husband had been a drug dealer and addict. We were always isolated and I longed to go out in the world. A simple day at the movies was blissful. There were also the big things I found very sexy. Burt had a great job, seemed ambitious, wanted to save money for the future, and claimed to be careful with money. After being married to someone reckless, I longed for these attributes. I was easily fooled.

The ambition that I thought he had in the beginning of our relationship, when he talked about his big plans, ended up really being procrastination. Sometimes things are not at all as they seem. The changes are gradual in the beginning. You hardly know they're happening. Before long, you're married to a stranger. What's worse, you've almost entirely lost yourself. You're a stranger, too.

I remember the first night he slept on the couch.

"Please go to the doctor," I pleaded. He just ignored me. He had already refused to go to the doctor but I persisted. "Maybe they can give you something or help you create a nutrition plan. The snoring only got this bad after the weight gain. It might be a hormone problem that they can address."

"I'll just sleep downstairs since it bothers you so much."

We had only been married for three and a half years. Had I known that moment would change our lives forever, maybe I would have fought harder, or given up faster. For the last 12 years of our marriage, we never slept together. That night the end of intimacy had begun. I still remember acquiescing:

"Fine, if you want to sleep on that lumpy old thing, don't let me stop you."

We went from having sex weekly to every second or third week. In the last four years of marriage, I was lucky if we did it four times a year. I still can't believe I let it go on that long. I also can't believe I didn't see how passive-aggressive he had become. His attitude was even worse than the physical distance. He abandoned me. It was so slow and subtle. I became nothing, of no importance. I had no identity. I was just there.

Burt had been sleeping in the living room for years before I realized he was actually living there. The couch was his home. And it was just as dysfunctional as our marriage. He had started playing computer games from 5:30 pm until about 1:00 to 2:00 in the morning, five nights a week—and 16 hours straight on weekends. He went from 185 pounds to 385 pounds in about five years. When something happens over time, it's hard to see, it's hard to confront. I distinctly remember the day I started to realize, the day I started to wake up. I opened the door after a long day at work. Burt was sitting at his computer, fixated on the screen, eating a bowl of macaroni and cheese. I felt my anger bubbling up. I walked over and dropped my briefcase by his feet. He didn't even look up.

"Did you give Laura dinner?"

He shook his head.

"For Christ's sake, you didn't even think to fix your 10-year-old daughter something to eat for dinner."

He acted as if he hadn't heard me. I knew there was no dinner for me, either. I wanted to yell, to scream, but I stood there looking at the fat slob he had become. I felt nothing but contempt. I just walked away. I fixed Laura a can of soup and crackers, because it was all I had the energy for. Then I got into my lonely bed and cried. When I woke up the next morning, for the first time in years, I was wide awake.

I started discovering the massive financial debt his addiction to Internet gaming had created. I had to confront the truth. He was passive-aggressive, overweight, lazy, and unwilling to change. He had chronic low self-esteem, and I had developed low self-esteem too. I felt like I was drowning. He was sinking and pulling me down with him, and it took every bit of strength I had to pull myself up. I had to save myself. It was a matter of survival. Like everything before, nothing happened quickly. It's not easy leaving the father of your child.

I felt guilty for the divorce and how it impacted her at the age of 12, but I felt Laura would be better off with that poor excuse for a father out of the house. He had abandoned me and his daughter emotionally, physically, and mentally. The only times he would do anything for either of us was if he had something he wanted to bargain for, versus doing it just because it needed to get done. I thought about that damn bowl of macaroni many times and how he sat there eating it, staring at the screen, while Laura and I had to fend for ourselves. It came to epitomize our relationship. In Laura's eyes, I was responsible because I asked for the divorce. I was the one who said I wasn't in love anymore. I feel that on days like today, when we are forced to be cordial for her sake. But there was no choice. I wasn't waving, I was drowning[1]. I was fucking drowning.

I feel so little for him now, I hardly think of him at all. Yet, standing there only feet away, with Laura beaming with optimism as she pledged her life to the man she loves, I did somehow relive it all, in a blink. When the nostalgia passed, and I saw Burt as he is now, I felt glad that I saved myself and only sorry I didn't do it sooner. Laura may never fully understand, because the overweight, lazy version of him is all she has ever known. She doesn't understand I married someone who no longer exists. I did everything I could to keep it going, but I was not going to throw away the one life I have. He was sinking and pulling me down with him. I wanted to save him too, but sometimes there's a choice to be made. I think when you're drowning, when you feel the waves crashing over you, something happens and you find out who you are. You either sink, or fight to stay afloat.

NOTE

[1] In *Reviving Ophelia: Saving the Selves of Adolescent Girls* (1994) therapist and author Mary Pipher describes her client Charlotte by saying, "I'm not waving, I'm drowning (p. 45)."

SARA

59 years old
Heterosexual
Caucasian
Religion not given

TUG-OF-WAR

When I was little, I worshiped my sister, Margaret. She was six years older and I desperately wanted to emulate her. As the oldest of four girls, she was the princess of her dominion. It seemed that everyone in the house looked up to her, but no one more so than me. I thought she possessed a magical quality that somehow made the sun shine brighter around her. Her wishes always seemed to come true. To me, she had it all. I projected all kinds of good qualities onto Margaret. I wanted to be popular, beautiful, and just like her.

Many of my happiest childhood memories were with Margaret. Sometimes we would have long talks that made me feel really important in her life. She told me about her dreams, secrets about boys, and even complained about our other siblings. I thought I was her favorite. I cherished those moments. But the good times were tempered with the bad. As important as she could make me feel in one moment, later she would be gone with her friends and I'd feel totally insignificant.

"John likes me, and he's told all my friends, but I'm still going to make him sweat it out more," she said as she set her pin curls. "I have to look good because I'm seeing him later."

"Is he cute?" I asked from bed, where I always lay while she prettied herself at the vanity.

"He's the most popular boy in my grade," she said as she fidgeted with her hair. "Don't tell anyone, but eventually when I agree to go out with him, I'm gonna let him feel me up."

I giggled, unsure of what to say but relishing the secret.

"How do I look?" she asked turning to me.

"Pretty. I love your hair, Margaret. I wish I had hair like that."

"Well, come here and let me fix yours. I'll make you look like a princess."

I eagerly hurried over. She got up and let me sit in her special chair, looking at myself in the beveled glass mirror atop her vanity, which I coveted. "Can you make curls at the bottom of mine too?" I asked, holding my hair in my hand.

"I promise I'll make it look magical."

I couldn't stop smiling. Not a moment after she touched my head the doorbell rang. "Oooh, I gotta go. My friends are here. Don't tell Mom we're going out with boys. Cover for me," she said as she scurried out before I could say goodbye. I sat in her chair a few minutes, looking in the mirror, wishing she had fixed my plain Jane hair and wondering if I was her friend too.

As these incidents increased, I also started to notice she got special treatment at home. She took advantage of that too. Everyone in the house made concessions for Margaret. I don't remember her carrying the same amount of responsibility for chores, and she always seemed to do things on her time. She made everyone wait for her and flaked out on a lot of commitments. I came to see her as selfish and narcissistic. She continually looked after her best interests, which often created circumstances where I was dumped for someone or something that would be more fulfilling to her. This happened time and time again. I kept forgiving her, especially when she was being the Margaret I thought she was, the one I wanted to emulate. Then, in very short order she would dump me again. It was like Charlie Brown and Lucy. Just as I would begin to trust her again, she would pull the football away.

I realize that being so much younger than her, I may have missed a lot. Maybe things weren't as imbalanced in our house as I perceived them to be. And now I can imagine how a teenager would prefer her peers over her younger sister. Maybe it wasn't as personal as it felt. None of that matters now. After what she did when my parents died, I know she is not trustworthy. It has been almost 10 years since I've seen or spoken to Margaret. I don't want to communicate with her. I don't want to know her. To understand what happened when my parents died, I have to go back to when I was about 11, a year before Margaret moved out of our house to go to college.

Mom wanted a dining room table that was big enough to seat our whole family, 11 of us in total. I think as my older siblings started leaving the house, the thought of holiday meals around a big table became more meaningful to her. It was hard to find a table that big, let alone one that we could afford. Mom dragged me from one antique dealer to another looking for the perfect table. One day we went to look at an antique dining table at a neighbor's house. I fell in love with this table. It was dark mahogany, stained with the slightest hint of red, my favorite color. The legs were intricately carved and the vast surface was so glossy I tried to see my reflection. I was elated when my mom bought that table. I told her then and there that I wanted it to be passed on to me someday.

My attachment only grew with every family dinner, special occasion, or holiday spent sitting around that beautiful table. Over time the table represented Bobby and Margaret visiting from college, something I looked forward to nearly as much as Christmas itself. My last memories with our beloved grandparents also happened around that table. It was always piled with casserole dishes, roast turkeys big enough to feed our neighborhood, and cinnamon-scented pies that I helped Mom make. That table was the locus of our best family times, from singing holiday songs to fighting over the last biscuit. It was the place we were all together. I dreamt of the day my own family would sit around that table. I was sure my family would be even better, without the sibling rivalry that at times crept into even the most beautiful holiday meals. That glossy mahogany reflected the best of my family, and my fantasies about the future. I loved it.

When my parents died, the day came for the precious family objects to be dispersed. The family picked cards to see who would go first, second, third, and so on. My brother Bobby, the oldest, got to pick first. He chose a desk he'd been wanting for a very long time. Next it was Margaret's turn. You guessed it. She chose my table. Everyone was shocked. For more than 40 years everyone knew that I had my heart set on having that table. I was devastated. The wound may not have been as deep had another of my siblings taken the table. It hurt more because she was the one. The depth of betrayal is tied to the depth of feeling. Admiration is the highest praise, and oh how I had admired her. I have not talked to Margaret since that day.

KEISHA

36 years old
Sexual orientation not given
African American
Non-denominational

HUSH

Father Mike's sermon was powerful. As usual, I sat quietly in the back but I swear I almost smiled when he warned about judging others. "Let he who judges another be judged himself." He brought it home with a message of compassion, and a reminder that we never know what another may be struggling with. I felt like he was talking about me. He was asking for compassion for me. He could hear my prayers, my inner thoughts. I was seen.

These days I usually slink out right away but I wanted to stay to thank Father Mike. I stood in the corner watching children in their Sunday best, girls with ribbons in their hair, running around as their parents socialized. Women were tag-teaming Father Mike, singing the Lord's praises and his. He's such a handsome man. So beloved. I waited patiently in the back. I don't like to socialize in church anymore, knowing what they think of me. When I sued that woman after the car accident and she falsely accused me of being a drug addict, people started treating me differently. Even my fellow church members and some of my friends act differently towards me now, as if I'm not trusted.

The woman I sued tried to deflect attention off of her own actions and call my credibility into question to avoid paying damages. She only accused me of drug use because of my teeth. I guess she took one look at me and figured people would be suspicious. I always knew my dental issue would haunt me. Due to an inherited condition, my teeth started decaying about eight years ago. At first it didn't bother me too much, but as it got worse I realized that many people would focus on my mouth rather than what I had to say. I've tried everything. I bought partial dentures a couple of times, but sometimes they shift while I'm talking or trying to eat. There's nothing I can do. My mouth is disgusting and it's become a huge part of my identity. It feels pretty bad when something you're embarrassed about is used against you. It was hard enough before, but now people think it's my own fault, like I'm a low-life. I was even willing to take a drug test and a lie detector test. Now I just keep to myself.

Just before Father Mike made his way over, Sally came charging at me, holding a pie wrapped in plastic wrap. You could see Sally from clear across town, always in a bright skirt suit or dress with a matching hat. Today she was dressed head to toe in red. How strange that they all saw me in scarlet.

"Well, Keisha. Look at you here in the corner. You practically blend into the background. Good, at least you came. The Lord forgives."

I didn't know how to take that. I was wearing a nice skirt and powder blue blouse, like I wear to church every Sunday. "Your pie looks good, Sally. What kind is it?"

As soon as I spoke I could see her eyes focus on my mouth. I barely open my mouth when I talk, sometimes people even ask me to speak up. This is why. The way they stare at my mouth affects my confidence almost all the time.

Before Sally replied, Father Mike made his way over to us. I wanted to say hello but hesitated. I smiled with my mouth shut as Sally handed him the pie.

"Father Mike, this is my peach pecan crumble, which I know you love. This time I used light brown sugar and a bit of maple." I wondered if she might pause, but she just continued on. "The sermon today, well you were speaking my language. I felt so inspired that . . . "

I slunk out as Sally continued bombarding Father Mike with compliments. The walk home was demoralizing. I had really wanted to thank Father Mike. I hope he didn't think I was rude; I just felt too self-conscious.

I got home to an empty house. I'd left Charee money to take everyone out for pancakes. With five children I don't get much time to myself. I changed into sweats and warmed up some leftover casserole. I know I have an overeating problem. It comes out when I'm stressed. When I was a young child, I was sexually assaulted. I didn't tell anyone for fear of what they would think. I learned how to go mute, and that's when my overeating started.

I sat on the couch, flipped on the TV and started eating, each bite of casserole bringing me a little comfort. Church, Sally, and all those judgmental people seemed further away.

I started to feel better when a Weight Watchers commercial with Jennifer Hudson came on. I used to identify with her, but she dropped out of the big girl club. I thought she had been happy with who she was, but she dropped all her curves. I knew I could stand to lose a couple of pounds but I liked the fact that I have curves and I'm thick in the right places. Beyoncé, Halle Berry, and Angelina Jolie represent the mainstream image, as if it's normal. The plus size figure is not respected. Some big girls are getting recognition too, like Monique, Gabourey Sidibe, and Queen Latifah, but it's still hard. The world looks at me as lazy. I was thinking about all of this when the door flung open. They all came barging in and disrupted the chatter in my head.

My little ones came running over to give me hugs. I smiled widely. Every day I try to focus on my loving kids, who trust and love me regardless of my flaws. Soon they start arguing over a toy that came with their food. "Hush, now. You all go and play nicely," I told them.

Charee, my 17-year-old daughter, walked over and handed me a Styrofoam container with leftover pancakes.

"I brought these for you."

"Thanks. Did everyone eat?"

"Uh-huh."

"Even you?" I ask.

Charee rolled her eyes. She wants to be a model and I worry deeply, because her body doesn't look healthy. I wanted to say something. I wanted to open my mouth, but before I could, she walked away. I never find my voice in time. It always hides. I opened the container of pancakes, berating myself as I took a bite. I lack self-confidence.

ELEANOR AND MARY

Eleanor
59 years old
Lesbian
Caucasian
Religion not given

Mary
59 years old
Sexual orientation not given
Caucasian
Religion not given

Sometimes when I see myself in the mirror, sometimes when I see myself through others' eyes... I don't like my appearance. I think an enormous number of women feel inadequate, and make themselves sick and miserable trying to measure up to standards that have no relationship to reality.

Eleanor

I do not like looking in mirrors and feeling unattractive... part of what makes me suffer is the mismatch of how I feel I look and then the mirror's confrontation.

I find I judge myself in terms of the appearance of others. I feel jealous and that's kind of terrible to feel.

Mary

MIRROR MIRROR

Eleanor

If the hotel lobby is any indication, the conference will be packed. I hope it trickles into my book signing. Sometimes I think women are afraid to be seen buying a book about female orgasm. Pretty sad. We can't even be interested in our own bodies without shame. Hmm... which way is my room? This place is like a maze. God, I hope Mary turns out to be a decent roommate. Rooming with a stranger is always scary. Just let me feel safe. Please don't let her be a homophobe. It's exhausting being guarded all the time. She seemed fine on email, but I'll bet she says something about my appearance. Why do they always think they can do that? It's so invasive. I'm butch, get over it. Hold up, Eleanor. Don't get ahead of yourself. Just because the last one was bad doesn't mean Mary will be. Don't prejudge her. Maybe she'll be swell. Give her a chance. Ah, here's the room.

***

Mary

Maybe I shouldn't have unpacked before Eleanor is here. I hope she's not offended I took the bed by the window. I don't know if she gets up in the middle of the night so I was trying to be considerate giving her the bed by the bathroom. What if she thinks it's rude? I don't know why I get nervous in these situations. For Christ's sake, Mary, you preach empowerment to women. And she seemed nice over email. I'm giving so many lectures at the conference I'll hardly be in the room anyway. It'll be fine. I'm curious too. Her work is so bold. I wonder what she looks like. She's probably a powerhouse. She'll probably look at me like a little old lady compared to her. Oh my goodness, I think she's here.

***

Eleanor and Mary

"Hi, you must be Eleanor. I'm Mary. Welcome."

"Nice to meet you, Mary."

"I hope you don't mind I took this bed. I left the drawers over there empty."

"Okay, thanks. I'm going to try to unpack quickly, before I go down to the book exhibit."

"I have to confess that when I put my name in the conference roommate-finder portal, I was a little worried about who I would get matched with. I've experienced a range in the past, but I do like to share hotel costs when I speak at these conventions. As soon as they sent me your information I looked you up and was blown away by your latest book. Holy moly!"

"Common reaction, Mary. Most people don't expect someone our age, let alone someone who looks like me, to write about female orgasm."

"True, people don't think women our age care about orgasms. I'm curious, do readers expect you to be younger? When you give talks at conventions like this are people generally surprised by what you look like?"

"Probably some are. I'm fairly certain that most people who see me on the street assume that I am an asexual kind of person, both because I look butch and because I look older. I doubt anyone pegs me for a sex and intimacy expert."

"How do people react when they find out about your work?"

"Most are surprised. Some are curious, others seem frightened off."

"Is it hard to, you know, meet people?"

"The fact that I have so many opinions about sex intimidates people who might otherwise be interested in dating, I think."

"I can see that, Eleanor."

"To be honest, though, the age thing puts women off too. Maybe more than anything else. Fifty-nine is tough."

"It sure is. I don't usually talk about this with people, I can't in my circles, but as I'm nearing 60 I feel pretty terrible about the way I look."

"What bothers you, Mary?"

"I'm 20 pounds heavier than I'd like to be. Some women look like a young 60, but I feel like the extra pounds make me more matronly."

"My body isn't as trim as it once was either, Mary, and sometimes I miss that."

"I felt bad about my weight most of my life. I remember starting to feel this way when I was around eight. People can say such cruel things. I remember being told 'nobody loves a fatty,' and 'you'd be so pretty if you lost weight.' I've been on a diet, or off a diet ever since."

"That's awful. I'm sorry."

"Eleanor, can I tell you something I've never told a soul? A few years ago I went through the horrible realization that even if I were able to lose the weight I'd struggled with since I was a girl, I'd still have wrinkles and look old."

"I'll bet most women our age can relate. An enormous number of women feel inadequate and make themselves miserable. When you look like me, you learn the importance of self-acceptance early on. I mean, I'm a butch dyke—butcher than any of those portrayed on TV, as you can see. So it's not like I buy into the toxic pop culture where women are portrayed as automatons. But the age thing even gets me. Sometimes when I see myself in the mirror, or when I see myself through others' eyes, I feel bad about the way I look."

"Oh, Eleanor, I don't like looking in mirrors either. Seeing someone unattractive looking back is terrible. Part of what makes me suffer is the mismatch of how I feel I look and the mirror's confrontation."

"Exactly."

"How I imagine I look to others is even worse. My husband doesn't know this because he would focus on why I care how other men see me, but about four years ago I had the 'invisible experience.' That was incredibly painful. As I've aged, the number of men who notice me has dwindled, but now it's as if they would rather not see me at all. It doesn't matter that I have a spouse. There's a profound feeling of loss, of erasure, when it becomes clear men are not open to the flirting I have done most of my life."

"For me, I feel like I am seen, but it isn't necessarily me they are really seeing. It's a stereotype, it's the one-dimensional version they want me to be. Men react to any butch dyke with fear. I'm not seen as a 'real' woman, whatever that means. And women can be just as judgmental."

"How do you find women judgmental?"

"Well, my usual style for dressing is very tough, casual, and what most people consider masculine. You can't entirely tell in this environment, because when I'm working I always make an attempt to look soft and try to tone it down so I don't alienate people. But even though my style is very butch, it's fun to dress up sometimes, and occasionally I would like to dress more femininely. The main reason I don't is because I'm afraid of the comments I would get from friends who see me as a butch lesbian, and want to keep seeing me as a butch lesbian."

"It seems no matter what we look like, and what our style is, we have to contend with the expectations of others. Don't you think, Eleanor?"

"We internalize those expectations, too. For the most part I really do like to wear casual things like old jeans, which fit my daily lifestyle, but I do wonder sometimes if I really dress the way I do because it makes me feel stronger and less likely to be harassed or attacked in some way. These fears and stereotypes go very deep."

"I hope you take this the right way, but it's comforting to know that I'm not alone."

"You said before that you never really share this with anyone, Mary. I guess I don't, either. I'm used to talking to women about their bodies and sexual identities, but I keep my own mostly to myself."

"I'm sure you'll relate; in my line of work, where I have a platform to coach others, I don't feel able to share these dark realities. I don't want to disappoint them, or diminish my message, even if I can't live up to it. I feel like the world sees me as a confident person and it's mostly inside that I suffer."

"If we could only block out how we think others see us, I wonder if we would see ourselves differently."

"Oh, Eleanor, I just noticed the time. We should probably get down to the conference."

"To give women empowerment lectures kind of makes you smile, doesn't it? All those eyes on us. You know, they will see us as strong and confident, Mary."

"If only I saw myself through their eyes."

"Isn't that the problem?"

***

Mary

Eleanor is remarkable. When I saw her, I never would have guessed we'd have anything in common. She's right that there's no one like her on TV. She's so masculine. I feel badly for how I judged her when she walked into the room. I was intimidated. I guess in some ways I'm one of those judgmental women she was taking about. That's hard to admit. I hope it wasn't obvious. Okay, focus Mary. Women who admire you are waiting. You need to be what they want to see. Get your head in the game.

***

Eleanor

Mary looks great for her age. Too bad she has such a hard time accepting herself. Who says to a girl, "Nobody loves a fatty" and "You'd be pretty if you lost weight." What's wrong with people? How is any girl supposed to feel good about herself? But God, if she only knew the things they said to me. Her skin would crawl. Try having, "Ugly dyke, I hope you die," screamed at you on the playground or muttered under the breath of men on the subway. There are so many times I've prayed to have the invisible experience. For her it's erasure; for me it would be survival.

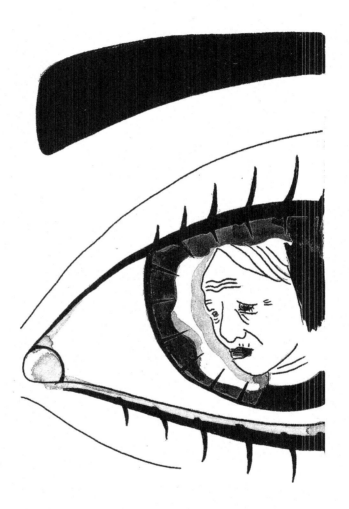

EMMA

41 years old
Heterosexual (now)
Caucasian
Religion noted as "all"

I was a doormat and try to placate him as well as I could. I felt like a terrible person and that I was just getting what I deserved. We were basically losers who wanted to be winners but were so wrapped up in ourselves, we didn't look for a way out.

Toxic — neither of us had any tools for coping with stress, challenge, heartache, you name it. We were quiet and resentful and angry. But addicted to one another in a needy, sick way.

Emma

WELCOME

TOXIC SOULMATES

When Susan called to tell me that Peter had died, I felt like I was hit by a truck. I hadn't seen him in more than 20 years, but I was instantly overcome with grief. My first thought was that it must've been suicide, which he had threatened many times. I was silent on the phone until Susan filled the space.

"Cancer," she said.

"What?"

"He had lung cancer. He put up a good fight but . . . "

"He never took a care of himself. All the smoking and drinking. I guess it caught up with him," I said.

"I'm so sorry, Emma. I didn't know if I should tell you. Bob didn't think I should, but I remember how in love you two once were. I thought you'd want to know before hearing about it from someone else."

"Thank you for telling me. It's shocking to even hear his name. It was a long time ago. I don't think about him anymore."

"Because I introduced you to each other, I felt I should be the one to tell you. Bob and I lost touch with Peter years ago, but we still have some friends in common and so I hear things. He never married or— "

"Well, thank you for telling me."

"I'm truly sorry, Emma."

"I'm fine. I'll talk to you soon."

After we hung up I leaned against the wall trying to breathe. *It was only a two-year relationship, more than 20 years ago, get yourself together,* I told myself. *It was toxic. He was toxic. I was a mess with him. It makes no difference to my life whether he's alive or not. I'm married to the man of my dreams now, this doesn't affect me.* I kept telling myself these things over and over again, but it was easier to lie to Susan than it was to lie to myself.

Matt came home that night and it was as if nothing happened. We ate dinner, talked about our day, watched television, and went to sleep. I never said a word to him about Peter. The heart is a deep and paradoxical reservoir. There was no reason to trouble the waters.

The day of Peter's funeral was emotional. I needed to be alone. He had great potential, but from what was posted online, he never amounted to much: no family, no money. The memorial must have been small and sad. I intended to spend the day working, but I stared at a blank Word document, consumed with memories of Peter. I remembered the moment we met as if it were yesterday.

"Emma, this is Peter, the writer I told you about. Peter, Emma is a grad student and aspiring writer."

"Nice to meet you, Emma," he said in a smooth voice as he outstretched his hand.

"You too," I mumbled as I shook his hand, afraid he would notice how sweaty my palm was.

Soon we were talking about philosophy, sharing our dreams, and laughing hysterically. He was sarcastic and funny. He was kind of an intellectual bad boy and that was sexy as hell. I was instantly in lust.

We became inseparable. We were everything-or-nothing people. I hung on every word he said, opening my mind and body fully. We debated philosophical ideas, watched arthouse films, spent hours writing at coffee shops, and made love with our eyes locked onto each other. I had never known such intense beauty. I was fully alive. He gave me the attention and approval that I had long craved. And as much as I tied myself to him, he also needed me, I thought. We were each other's entire universe.

When we couldn't bear to be apart, I even allowed him to live with my mother and me, without really checking with my mom. I let it happen. That was a part of my pattern in those days, getting swept away and letting things happen. Life was a garden growing wildly with no gardener tending it. I was convinced I had met my Prince Charming and became completely entangled in him and the dream of us.

The beautiful summer days filled with possibility soon turned cold, gray, and desolate. Neither of us had any tools for coping with stress, challenge, heartache, you name it. If he got a rejection, or I got a poor grade in school, or if there was a problem with a friend or relative, everything would blow up. It could've been anything. He once got angry that I took an extension from a professor on an assignment. She had offered it because she needed my help on something, and gave it to me in lieu of my leaving to work on the assignment. Somehow this caused us to fight. Peter was furious. It spiraled. I yelled at him. He yelled at me. And then we were quiet, resentful, and angry. At some point I realized he was competitive with me, and vice versa. We both aspired to be amazing, but didn't really know what that meant nor did we have any tools to get there.

He started going out with people I didn't know, coming home at all hours, and sleeping all day. If I asked about his plans to write, he became defensive and attacked me. In truth, nearly everything I said was antagonistic or passive-aggressive. I was just as dysfunctional as he was, expressed in the opposite way. We lived in a state of quiet resentment, or yelling and making snide remarks, or active and passionate lovemaking. It was nothing or everything.

We were addicted to one another in a needy, sick way. We thrived on the dysfunction because we didn't know any alternative. I rarely knew where I stood with him, where the relationship was going, and yet it was all I cared about. I think he actively tried to keep me feeling insecure in the relationship to make himself powerful, and to keep a hold on me. I was addicted to the chase, the uncertainty, the despair. I mistook it for romance. We were so lost in self-deception, depression, and other terrible habits that we had no chance at happiness on our own, much less together. We were basically losers who wanted to be winners, but we were so wrapped up in ourselves we didn't look for a way out.

Finally it got to be too much. I was standing at the edge of the precipice and it seemed as if he wanted to push me over. Maybe he wanted out too, but didn't know how to do it. He was reading my thesis, which he'd promised to copyedit. He took far longer than he had promised and I was afraid of missing the due date. I pushed him to finish. One day when I was working, he approached me and dropped my thesis on my desk so aggressively the pages scattered. From the first page I could see it was bleeding with his red ink. He crossed out nearly the entire first page and wrote, "Derivative," in the margin.

Clearly, he wanted to hurt me. He could be very mean. It was subtle but cut to the bone. His comments were often in the guise of helping me. If I didn't take them well he claimed I was just "over-sensitive" and would never "make it as a writer." It was always very hard to pinpoint his motives but the energy was terrible.

He spent the next 20 minutes ripping my thesis to shreds, and haranguing me for not being a better thinker and writer. His words haunted me for many years and made me even more insecure than I already was. At the time I got angry and lashed out in return, berating him for being a loser who was never going to make anything of himself. I broke up with him, but went back.

By the end we were both violently bitter. We knew we had to sever all ties. Leaving him was the hardest thing I ever did. As toxic as our relationship was, without that energy I was completely lost. I worried I would be alone for the rest of my life. I felt like I was a terrible person and that I was just getting what I deserved.

No matter how hard I tried, I couldn't seem to get over him. For some time I was really rattled. The relationships that eventually followed were just as bad, but never to that depth. When I found myself in a similar relationship, I got out in two months instead of two years. I even dated a woman, thinking that I might be a lesbian since I couldn't make it work with men. Again, a morose and sad affair of two well-intending people who had no tools. It all came down to an overwhelming fear of not being enough. I always thought, *if this person likes me, at least someone likes me*. Often the only criterion was that they asked me out, or were interested. Over and over again, I settled. But Peter was always the one I couldn't quite get over. For years I wondered if we were soulmates, meant to be together, but too screwed up to make it work.

I'm not still in love with him, or even with the idea of him, and I haven't been for many years. But that relationship brought me to my knees. All the frustration, fear, and anger brought me down to the point where I had no place to go but up. From the ashes rose the phoenix, and now I get to use my mess as my message. In some strange way, Peter is the subtext in all of my books. I never would have become a writer, a wife, or anything else without having survived him.

I learned a lot about myself and it helps me to be empathetic towards others. It's incredible how far I have come. Had it not been for him, I don't think I would've ever learned that I deserve the best—as does everyone on this planet. Maybe that's why I feel this profound sadness at his passing. I'm not romanticizing the days when in fact I was an insecure, irrational doormat. I think I'm mourning the death of the Prince Charming idea, the shortness of Peter's troubled life, and that sad little girl who had no tools.

CHAPTER 12

KAYLA

59 years old
Lesbian
Caucasian
Religion noted as "eclectic"

Without ever thinking about it, I curtailed my life and my own needs on her behalf. It was an unquestioned assumption about what was necessary if I was going to be in an intimate relationship.

On a deep level, I believed I had to settle.

It's what I saw my mother doing to my father.

Kayla

PIECES OF MYSELF

October 5

I heard that Shelley and her partner are getting married now that it's legal. I want to be happy for her, I do. It's been more than 10 years. But some wounds, some regrets, linger. I still feel hurt. It's funny because Jaime and I were together for just about five years too, just like Shell and I, and when we split she found someone else right away and I didn't care. I know that's what people say to save face, but it's the truth. Of course, we had led fairly separate lives and only saw each other on weekends. I knew I could not be there for her the way she wanted and I needed to let her find someone else who could, and I needed to be free. With Jaime I could be happy for her. And we also still love each other, insofar as we ever did. But Shelley . . . Shelley was the love of my life. I know that regrets are pointless and we can only learn, grow, and try to do better for ourselves and others, but I still miss her.

When my friend told me about Shelley's engagement, I guess she saw the look in my eyes. I tried to conceal it. Naturally, she asked about our relationship. What was I going to say? It was the most expanding relationship of my life. She really brought out the best in me. She didn't let me hide. She really helped me to step fully into my own being-ness, and get in touch with my own needs, with my power, with myself. I became a better version of myself because of her, but not without a lot of pain. I knew if I said any of that she would ask how it ended, so I just said that we were really in love and it was a special time, long ago.

October 6

Last night I couldn't stop thinking about Shelley, about our relationship. I lay awake in bed for hours. I think I was afraid to go to sleep and dream about her. It's scary when something you had so many years ago is the yardstick by which you inadvertently measure everything else. Nothing can live up to it. But when I finally fell asleep, it was my parents who haunted me. The same recurring, surreal, memory-dream. The whole thing unfolded in slow motion.

I'm six years old, wearing a little black-and-white plaid sundress. I'm sitting on the floor of my room holding Mr. Teddy and telling him what happened to me when Uncle Tom came over. I hear my teddy bear talking back to me, encouraging me to tell my mommy. I want to tell, but it's so hard for me to speak up. I finally gather up my courage and take Mr. Teddy's hand and start walking to the kitchen to find Mommy. But as I approach the kitchen I hear my father yelling:

"If I say I'm going out, then I'm going out."

"I only wanted to know if you'll be home for dinner," my mother sheepishly replies.

"Just leave me a plate if I'm not back."

"I had hoped to, to . . . "

"What? What is it? Spit it out, I'm late."

Mommy doesn't say anything so he leaves, slamming the door behind him. I know what she wanted to ask him. Last time we were at the post office, she took a flyer about classes at the community center. She always reads the bulletin board, looking for something. She told me not to say anything about it until she could figure out the best way to ask Daddy. She's not good at asking for things.

By the time Teddy and I get to the doorway of the kitchen, she's standing over the sink staring at a pile of dirty dishes, with her head down. She looks sad. I open my mouth but no words come out. I desperately want to speak but I can't. I'm mute. I turn around and go back to my room before she notices me.

Usually when I have this dream, I wake up in a cold sweat, wrapped in a mix of memories of Tom, the violation, and all the silence. Therapy helped a lot, but when the dreams come, it's awful all over again. This time was different, though. I found myself thinking about my mother. I only now realize it's like she put everything she wanted in life high up on a shelf, out of sight, collecting dust. I think she put the pieces of herself up there one by one, so maybe she didn't notice, but eventually that shelf was piled high. When you pile it up that high, and lose that many pieces of yourself, it's bound to come crashing down. I know that I did the same thing with Shelley. I tried to change who I was to be with her and it only tore us apart. The crazy thing is that she was nothing like my father. She didn't want me to change myself for her, but I didn't know that. Without ever thinking about it, I curtailed my life and my own needs on her behalf. It was my unquestioned assumption about what was necessary if I was going to be in an intimate relationship.

October 18

Shelley is getting married today. There's a part of me that felt hurt not being invited, which is madness since we haven't seen or spoken to each other in many years. I wouldn't go, anyway. Can't think of anything more unbearable. Yet it makes me feel left behind, again. Such an important day in her life and I'm not a part of it. I remember the day she told me about Lisa like it was yesterday. I should've known it was the beginning of the end, although she would probably say the beginning to our end was long before that. And it was.

I was sitting at the kitchen table writing in my journal when she came in. That's not where I normally did my writing, but I had stopped in the kitchen to brew another pot of coffee and it was bright and sunny in there that day, so I decided to sit at the table and continue writing while I waited for the coffee. It was so unremarkable when I heard the apartment door close, and Shelley drop her bag, that I just continued writing. Not a moment passed and she was standing in the doorway of the kitchen.

"Hey. Can I talk to you?"

I was right in the middle of trying to get a thought down and I knew I would lose it but I said, "Sure. I'm making coffee."

Shelley sat in the seat adjacent to mine. I closed my journal with my pen keeping my place and Shelley reached her hand out to me. She placed her hand gently on top of mine. I had a knot in my stomach.

"Kayla, I started seeing someone else."

I instinctively withdrew, folding my hands across my lap, sitting in silence.

"I promised you if this happened I would be open about it. Her name is Lisa. She—"

"No, please don't. Please don't tell me about her. Not now. I only want to know one thing, that it's just sex. It isn't anything more than that, it can't be. Nothing between us has to change."

I could see the frustration on Shelley's face as she replied, "If things between us hadn't changed then there wouldn't be anyone else. I only wanted you but . . . "

"But I can't give you everything you need. I know that. But sex is such a small part of our relationship, if you need to get that one part from her, I will try to live with it."

"It wasn't a small part in the beginning. Have you forgotten?"

"I know I withdrew sexually."

"We haven't been intimate for three years, Kayla."

I had nothing to say. What could I say? So she continued.

"You knew eventually I would take a lover. We talked about it, we cried about it, we fought about it. I met Lisa and I instantly felt a connection to her. We have a deep attraction. She's passionate. I'm committed to truth and so you need to know."

"You're sleeping with her."

"Yes."

"Does she know about me?

"Yes."

"What did you tell her, that your girlfriend is asexual?"

"She knows about our situation. I still love you, and I'm still here. I'm not going anywhere. But I need a physical relationship."

"Do what you need to do, just still be here for me."

Shelley looked down, nodded and then went into another room. As she left, the coffee machine beeped and the buzzing seemed to reverberate in my mind, further etching the moment into my memory.

It took many months before we broke up. We tried to make it work, but she really fell for the other woman and I felt abandoned. Eventually, in order to pull myself together, I had to separate from her.

I think about it now, and my role in it, and I wish I knew then what I know now. From the beginning I had doomed us. It's ironic, because all I ever wanted to do was to make her happy. I was willing to do anything. I didn't go places I wanted to go because she didn't want to go. I didn't hang out with people I wanted to hang out with because she might get jealous. I curtailed my own life and my own needs on her behalf. As I chipped away the pieces of myself, those things created a certain level of resentment in me. That's what caused me to lose my desire for her. It was all occurring on a deeply subconscious level, but because of my history around childhood abuse I think it was instinct for me to withdraw physically when I wasn't happy. We never talked about it at the time, because I didn't realize what I was doing. The crazy thing is that she told me she had never wanted me to change myself on her behalf.

I wish I could've just been myself from the beginning. I think she may actually have loved me as I was. But on a deep level, I believed you had to settle in order to have a lasting relationship. It's what I saw my mother doing with my father. So I closed my mouth and tied myself up. The resentment grew and I had less and less to give her. It's no wonder she turned her back on me.

CHAPTER 13

RACHEL

59 years old
Heterosexual
Caucasian
Jewish

95

IRREPARABLE DAMAGE

Should I go to them? Should I run in and try to stop the fighting? Will it make it worse like last time? I'm so sleepy. I wish they'd stop yelling.

"I hate you, Ralph! You're a weak, pathetic excuse for a man!"

"Please stop screaming, Dana. You'll wake up Rachel. It's after midnight."

Oh no, why did Daddy do that?

"Rachel, Rachel, Rachel! The only reason I stay in this marriage is because of her!"

"Just stop shouting. Calm down."

"Don't tell me what to do!"

I can't take it anymore. She's not going to stop. Take a deep breath, Rachel. Be brave.

"I would leave you if not for Rachel. One day I will . . . "

I have to go now.

"You're being—"

"Mommy, Daddy, please, please don't argue," I beg as I burst into their room. I run into my mother's arms hugging her, which I feel is my responsibility. "Please stay together. I'm begging you." I cling tighter, trying to prove my love.

It's quiet and still. A moment of deceptive peace before one of her favorite games.

"Ralph, if the house were burning down, which one of us would you try to save first?"

My insides clench. *Don't fall for it, Daddy. Please don't answer.*

"Stop it. Stop trying to provoke something, Dana."

"Answer me, Ralph! Which one, me or Rachel?"

"Well, Rachel is a child."

I squeeze my eyes closed. *I wish he didn't pick me. This will throw her into a rage and she won't speak to him for days. And she'll hate me even more.* I brace for the inevitable.

I am 6 years old.

***

Oooh, I love mashed potatoes. And chopped meat, too. I wish she didn't put peas in it. I wonder if she'll notice if I pick them out.

"Put your napkin on your lap, Rachel."

"Yes, Dad."

He smiles. *Uh oh, Mom saw. I love Sunday dinner at the dining room table. Please don't be upset. I'm hungry.*

"Rachel, hand me your plate."

"Here it is, Mom." My mouth waters as the food plops down.

"Dana, can you please pass the potatoes?"

"Ralph, which one of us would you try to save first if the house were burning down?"

Oh no.

"Well, Ralph. Which one?"

"You, Dana. I would save you."

"Here are the potatoes, Ralph," she says with a shrewd smile. "Well Rachel, it looks like you'd just have to find your own way out of a burning house," she declares triumphantly. "Now eat your dinner."

"I'm not hungry."

I am 8 years old.

***

"I'm going to slit my wrists. Watch the blood drain from my body."

"Mom, please, stop saying things like that."

"You won't know when it's going to happen. You'll be at school. But I'll make sure you're the one to come home and find my body."

Stop it. Please just stop. Just stop!

"I'll leave a note for your father. He's the reason for my despair. When you realize how it's his fault you'll hate him forever."

"Dad loves you, Mom. I love you."

"I've never loved your father. It's better to be loved than to love in return. Go away now. Leave me alone. One day you'll see."

I am 9 years old.

***

"Can I try to flip one, Dad? They're bubbling like you said."

"Sprinkle the chocolate chips on the pancake first. Then let me show you how to hold the spatula so they don't land batter-side down on the floor."

As I flip one perfectly, I notice his pride. But not a moment later, there's a shimmer of trepidation in his dark eyes. He slinks back, increasing the distance between us. *She must be here.*

"Look over here, you two. Smile."

I turn to see Mom wielding her camera. A forced smile creeps on my face.

"Oh look, you burned one," she says, just as her finger snaps the picture.

"Dana, it's pretty early for you to be at it," Dad says, gesturing to her cup.

"Mind your own business."

I'm so glad she's capturing these Kodak moments through her alcoholic haze.

I am 10 years old.

***

God, I hate bringing friends home. This was a bad idea. Please don't let her embarrass me.

"Come on in, guys. You can put your shoes there and bring your backpacks up to my room."

"Your house is really nice, Rachel. It's like a real-life version of this beautiful dollhouse I had when I was little."

Dollhouses are haunted. "Thanks, Sara."

"Can we get a snack or something?"

"Yeah, a snack would be good."

Shit. I just want to get you to my room.

"Sure. Come to the kitchen but try not to be too loud. My mom may be sleeping."

"At three in the afternoon?"

"Uh, yeah. She uh, sometimes she naps when my dad is at work."

"We'll be quiet."

"The sodas are over there. Take what you want while I grab the chips."

"Rachel! Rachel, are you home?"

Oh no.

"Did we wake your mom up?"

"It's okay, Jody."

"Ah, you brought friends over," she says, peering into the room.

"Yeah, Sara's mom said our study group couldn't go there this time because they have a plumbing problem. Dad said we could come here."

"Did he?"

"We were just getting a quick snack and then we'll go to my room."

"Do you really think you should be eating greasy potato chips with your skin problems?"

Gee, thanks Mom. I already hate how I look. I'm so glad you said that in front of my friends. I just want to die.

"Did Rachel ever tell you how she tried to cure her acne with toothpaste and then couldn't get it off? It was hysterical."

Yeah, real funny, Mom. Thanks for mortifying me even more. At least they're not laughing. Maybe they feel bad for me. That'll probably piss her off.

"Don't be rude. Introduce me."

"This is Sara, and you've met Jody before."

"Oh yes, I remember. The one with divorced parents from the other side of town."

Oh my God. Why can't she just be nice like other mothers? It's bad enough she doesn't let Dad have friends. Sara and Jody probably hate me now.

I am 15 years old.

***

I'm finally getting out of this house of horrors. I'm never going to look back. I'm never going to speak to my mother again.

"Rachel, pursuing theater is absurd. You'll fail."

"It's my life, Mom. I'm going to live it."

"Ralph, she's probably an alcoholic lesbian or a drug addict."

Coming from the world's biggest lush, that's rich.

"You're not a good writer, Rachel. You'll never be the playwright you imagine. Get over it."

"Thanks for the encouragement, Mom."

"And that studio apartment you're moving into is too small."

"I can breathe there. It's small, but it's my own space. I can breathe there."

"Listen to your mother, Rachel."

Oh Dad, I lost respect for you long ago. But at least I'm the lucky one. I get to move away and never go back.

I am 19 years old.

***

"Honey, a registered letter came for you today. It's from an attorney's office."

I inhale, knowing in my soul it's from one of them. I hold it in my hands, reminding myself what a successful life I have built. I graduated with honors, I achieved the career I always dreamt of, I have friends, and for 14 years I've been married to a smart and wonderful man. I'm okay, somehow, despite my sad childhood. I learned how to comfort myself. I learned how to take care of myself. I learned how to live with intention. I can deal with this.

Dear Rachel,

I had my attorney locate you. I'm proud to learn you've done well in your life. Your mother's health is deteriorating. She no longer knows who I am. I've spent every day caring for her in a beautiful residential facility. She will die soon. I would like to come and visit you to pick up where we left off. You are the sole beneficiary of our estate and I don't know how long I have.

Your father.

"Well, what was the letter?"

"It's from my father. My mother is dying. He wants to see me, as if decades have not passed. He's oblivious."

"What are you going to do?"

"Send a letter via his attorney telling him I hope his remaining years are happy but it's not possible for us to ever reconnect."

"You should do whatever is right for you, and I support you. But are you sure?"

There's not a flicker of doubt in my heart. "I am. I always knew I had to cut the cord. Even as a little girl, the seeds had already been planted."

"For what?"

"Irreparable damage."

I am 59 years old.

YAEL

26 years old
Heterosexual
Caucasian
Jewish

CHAPTER 14

POTATO CHIPS

I think they're sagging even more. Maybe if I adjust my bra straps. I hate this. I'm only 26 years old. Eighteen months ago, when I first noticed my breasts started sagging a lot more, I thought maybe I was imagining it. But this is really happening. It's awful. Now I'm getting close to needing a breast lift. I hope I can save enough money to afford it by the time I'm 30. Hmm, if I hold them up where they should be they look . . .

"Yael? Are you upstairs?"

God, that startled me. "Yeah? What's up?"

"Honey, are you going for your morning walk or do you want coffee?"

"I'm walking for at least half an hour. I'll make my own coffee when I get back before my interview with that fashion blogger. Thanks."

"We should leave for the birthday barbecue at 3:00."

"Okay."

***

This is a bit depressing. I walk and walk, but nothing makes a difference. After years of feeling comfortable in my own skin, I'm starting to feel fat. I want to lose weight. I feel a little helpless because I try to take steps to look better, but they don't work. I guess it could be worse. I like my eyes and my face. And for my size, I have a pretty flat tummy. I should focus on what's good, make it work for me. Maybe I'll do another lap around the reservoir, make it a full hour today.

***

"Dylan, I made a fresh pot of coffee, if you want more. We're almost out of creamer."

"Thanks. I'm all set."

"Ugh, I hate these 'who wore it best' things. The youngest and thinnest always wins. It's predictable."

"Why do you read those magazines everyday if you feel that way? Seriously, Yael. That stuff isn't good for women."

"You know I mostly read fashion magazines for work. Every clothing designer has to stay on top of the trends. It's part of my job and I love it."

"Yeah, okay. I'm going to take a shower."

I hate talking about that stuff. What am I supposed to say? This is my work, but I also know what he means. Maybe he knows I'm in a bit of a funk because I want to slim down. He might have noticed I cut out regular soda. I guess I'm just struggling a bit. I love my job but it has a downside. I don't hate how I look, but more and more I've been feeling bad about not being smaller. I'm around a lot of models and I hear size 2 girls complain about dieting. It might finally be getting to me. I'm 5'2" and a size 10/12. I can barely fit in my own brand. I don't want to have to custom fit everything. I want to belong in my own demographic. I just can't dress the way I want. I think about it daily. It used to be much less. Maybe it is my business. I look at these magazines and the truth is I want to see the clothes on the best-looking body. Not too skinny or large. Even if it's not going to look that way on me. If it doesn't look perfect in the magazine, no one will want to buy it. Besides, Dylan is wrong. I'm not impacted by magazines or TV.

***

"Hi, Lisa. Thanks so much for featuring me on your blog. It's great for my business."

"My pleasure, Yael. I love your clothes. My blog focuses on the designer, as a way of bringing attention to the design house. So let's get started with the first question. Please describe your personal style."

"Tailored and polished with a slight pop of something a little funky and fresh, when dressing up. But most of the time I wear premium denim jeans and simple colored cotton tees—sometimes graphic tees. I love to accessorize for comfort and style." *Or to hide my flaws, but I'll keep that to myself.*

"What three words best categorize your personal style?"

"Classic, contemporary, sexy."

"What does your style say about you? What does it reflect about your personality, values or interests?"

Uh, maybe it says I'm a hypocrite. That's how I feel some days. Can't say that. "I think it reflects me very well. I am all of those things. However, I use clothes to accentuate the best parts and bring out the sexiest features."

"How typically 'feminine' do you consider your style?"

"I'm not typical. I think I use a lot of traditionally masculine styles and change them into something powerful and sexy."

"What kind of clothes/fashion do you normally wear?"

"I love well-tailored jackets and suits. I don't wear many dresses, but when I do, they are very detailed. I'm a huge fan of jeans and classic tees that you can jazz up."

"Is your personal style a big influence on your brand?

"Yes, absolutely. My style is reflected in my work." *Sadly I can barely fit into my work. I wish I was more like my customers.*

"Given your business, do you think women can get stuck in a certain look without exploring other parts of their personalities?"

"Yes. I think women tend to get comfortable in knowing what works for them in certain circumstances and always go to that look. Sometimes it's because of specific attention they get, and they want the same feeling and don't know how to do that with different looks. Sometimes it's self-image: they are afraid to try other looks due to one bad experience, or self-consciousness. I also know that how a garment looks on a hanger can be very misleading compared to how it fits. I'm lucky because I experience this from many different directions, and have figured out how to see past it. I have designed for a lot of women and when someone asks me to make them something custom, half the time I have to convince them to try something new. Otherwise, what's the point? They usually listen to me and are very happy about it."

"Any tips to women looking for new clothes?"

"Try things out to see if they are flattering. Never just assume. Hanger appeal is very misleading."

"Well, that should do it. That was great. Thank you."

"Thank you!"

***

"Come on, Yael. We're going to be late."

"It's a barbecue; it's okay to be late. I'll be ready soon. I'm still straightening my hair and I have to throw my clothes on."

"I'll sign Ruthie's card from us while I wait."

Why isn't my hair cooperating today? It's so frizzy. I hope it doesn't frizz up when we're outside. I wish I knew the best cut for my hair. Okay, some extra spray should do it. Now, what am I going to wear? When in doubt, jeans and a classic T-shirt. I can kick it up a notch with a silk scarf. Ooh, not this T-shirt. The neckline makes my breasts look even lower. Besides, it's too fitted. I'll look horrible if I eat carbs. I wish carbs weren't my weakness. Especially potatoes. I'm addicted to sugar and potatoes. They'll probably have potato chips at the barbecue. I won't be able to resist. I should wear a baggy shirt. I wonder if I look stocky in these jeans with flats on? I don't want to wear heels in their yard. I'm too short.

"Hey, Yael, you almost ready?"

"Oh God, you startled me."

"Well, I can see you're not ready."

"Sorry. I just need to put a top on."

"Or, you could leave it off and we could—"

"Don't even think about it. We're already late."

"I thought you said you couldn't be late to a barbecue?"

"And of course you pick now to listen to me. Here, I'm putting this shirt on and we can go."

"Let me take a picture. I can post it to Facebook and write a cute caption for Ruthie about how we're heading over."

"Um, not right now, okay?" *Don't you realize I really don't like being in photos anymore?*

"Come on, what's the biggie? You look beautiful. Just one picture?"

"Fine, okay."

I just hope he doesn't want to have sex tonight. I don't want to be looked at naked. I don't feel sexy. I'm sure I'll feel even worse if I binge on potato chips.

KATE

49 years old
Heterosexual
Caucasian
Agnostic

EVERYONE SETTLES

After spending another day at Howard's, I've reaffirmed that moving into his house is on indefinite hold. That family farmhouse is the definition of the word squalor. There's dirt and filth all over the place, not to mention some hoarding issues. Who keeps stacks of old magazines, junk mail, and outdated coupons piled high? Since he knows I won't move in until the house is cleaned to my satisfaction, I'm in no great danger of moving the relationship forward. He'll never fix that place.

I would also be in a constant state of frustration watching him interact with his kids. It's aggravating just hearing about it. He really isn't much of a parent. There are no boundaries, no rules, no consequences for the kids. He's the only parent they have, if you consider what a loser their mom is. But he rarely, if ever, embraces teachable moments, or parents with a firm hand. His kids walk all over him and treat him like a doormat. Meanwhile, he always tries to play the victim and act like he's helpless to change things. When I point out that he's acting like a victim, he gets defensive. Just a couple of weeks ago we had another argument about Jacob that confirmed things are never going to change. We were watching television when a commercial for Caribbean cruises came on.

"Looks beautiful. We should think about a vacation some time. We never go anywhere," I said.

"It's not a good time," he replied.

"I didn't mean we had to go now. But we could plan something."

"I'm really strapped right now. Jacob is hurting for money and asked me for a loan."

I sighed and rolled my eyes. I sat, seething, looking at him in disgust, too angry to even respond.

"It's not like the other times. His workplace has been on a two-week shutdown. I feel sorry for him," Howard sheepishly said.

"For Christ's sake, Howard, he's 20 years old and he still lives at home with his dad. Don't you think you do enough for him? How is he ever going to grow up?"

"He has a job, he just doesn't earn a lot of money. There's nothing I can do."

"His company shuts down every year. Jacob knew that in advance. He should've found himself a temporary job to tide him over until the company started back up."

"It's too late now, so there's no point in talking about it anymore."

We spent the rest of the night watching a Star Trek marathon. We usually quote lines to each other, but I was fuming. We watched in silence. I find his willingness to excuse bad behavior really aggravating. There is only so much I can do.

If I'm being completely honest, in some ways the cluttered house and obnoxious kids are a convenient excuse. The truth is, I prefer living alone.

I had lunch with my friend Jeanette the next day and she complained incessantly about the new guy she's seeing. She doesn't trust him. She caught him in what might've been a lie about whether or not he is dating other women. After that she became paranoid. When he was taking a shower she grabbed his cell phone to search through his texts and emails but it was password-protected. She spent the entire lunch vacillating between feeling guilty for invading his privacy and wondering if she should trust her gut.

"I mean, why is his phone password-protected? Don't you find that odd?" she asked.

"It's suspicious."

"It could be because of his work, though. You know, like protecting client information."

"Maybe. You could ask him."

"But if he's lying to me, then he'd just lie. How will I know?"

"I know exactly how you feel. In the beginning of my relationship with Howard there were issues of inappropriate behavior with his ex-girlfriend. While she clearly understood that she had broken up with him and didn't want to reconcile, he had trouble accepting that. The inappropriate behavior had to do with the tone of his emails to her, flirting with her and offering the kind of support that one generally offers a girlfriend, and keeping the extent of his end of the relationship secret from me. He once took her out for a motorcycle ride that he never told me about."

"That's awful," Jeanette said. "How did you find out about it?"

"I went through his emails. He was foolish enough not to delete things."

"It would've been worse if he deleted those emails. Then you never would've known. How did you deal with it?"

"I've done so much therapy and I've learned about communication. I've had to teach him. He knew nothing. After we fought about the ex, we both agreed on the importance of transparency. We try to talk to each other in a respectful way. I think we succeed nicely."

"Weren't your feelings hurt?"

"It's been quite a struggle over the years. When we got together, he had just come out of a 20-year marriage to woman who had become a drug addict and alcoholic. He brought some very negative attitudes to our relationship. He was really overdue for an attitude overhaul after his divorce. I think because of what he'd been through with his ex-wife I let some things slide in the beginning. After what happened with his ex-girlfriend I absolutely do not look the other way anymore, or make excuses."

"So, should I confront him with my suspicions or just try to figure out his damn password?"

We laughed and moved on to other things, but the conversation opened up old wounds.

I couldn't sleep that night. There are some things I didn't feel comfortable telling Jeanette. I couldn't stop thinking about it. Howard wasn't the only one at fault for the problems in our relationship. Sometimes I think Howard sought companionship with his ex because I was such a handful.

I also brought baggage and dysfunction to the relationship. I definitely had a pattern of making bad relationship choices. My first husband was a wife beater. My second husband was a nice guy with a huge amount of his own baggage. My next relationship was with a crack addict I was trying to save. I failed miserably, but at least I finally started working on saving myself.

It took repeated relationship disasters and years of therapy to realize that because I was molested by a family member for many years, I brought dysfunction to my relationships and made bad relationship choices. I've known other childhood sexual abuse survivors who, like me, tolerated bad relationships because they didn't have the self-esteem to see their own destructive patterns. Sexual abuse survivors in particular seem to settle for whoever will have them.

I guess the truth is, I'm still somewhere between never wanting to settle again and very much settling. That's why I'm still with Howard. We laugh, we hug a lot, and in some ways, the relationship suits me. It's neither too intense, nor too distant. But it's been four years and we don't live together and I don't want to live together. Very little of my identity is tied up in the relationship. I mean, he's not Eric Clapton. Now he would be my ideal! But if you have an ideal man in mind, and that ideal man is nonexistent or unattainable, then you're pretty much forced to settle for something less than what you really wanted. Doesn't everyone settle for what they can get?

On some level I am settling, which is why I guess I can take it or leave it. I try not to let this get in the way of enjoying what I do have, though. I don't know if there's anyone out there better for me, or if there's anyone out there better for him. All I know is that this relationship works for now.

CHAPTER 16

CRYSTAL

74 years old
Heterosexual
Caucasian
Roman Catholic

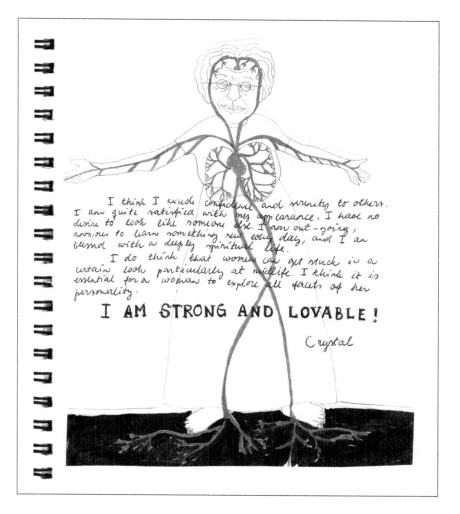

STRONG AND LOVEABLE

What to wear? What to wear? One should dress professionally. I have to look nice at my own book reading. Sorting through options in my closet, I must say I am the thrift shop queen. I have purchased suits, dresses, slacks, sweaters, and quality tops at ridiculously low prices. My Emmett would be proud if he could see me now. I'm still very feminine, not just for a 74-year-old woman, but period. I have no desire to look like someone else, including a younger version of myself. I'm under no illusions, nor do I want to be. Aging with dignity and dressing appropriately go hand in hand. Going out in shorts is a definite no-no. *Hmm, this is nice. A simple floral dress with a cardigan. Professional, but with pizzazz.*

Some authors are nervous when they walk into a bookstore to give a reading. After spending my career as a teacher, I have no fear of public speaking. Book talks are a privilege. Pop culture gives women a shelf life of 28 years. That's why my guidebook for maturing women is necessary. I am confident that my message will make an impact.

***

As people are shuffling in and taking their seats I can see the flyers posted at local coffee shops, my health club, and the senior center were effective. Soon nearly every seat is filled. I begin with a reading:

"Pop culture's portrayal of women as blonde, exceedingly thin, coated with makeup, with that come hither look is ridiculous! Just open up any magazine or go online and you have plenty of examples. Women have a choice. If you want the media, pharmaceutical and cosmetic companies running your life, then you will remain a victim. Pop culture is going to have to adjust its way of thinking because our Boomer Generation is now on the forefront."

Their cheers are ferocious. Now my favorite part, the Q&A.

A woman who I suspect is around my age, but has had too many Botox and collagen injections to safely guess her age, purses her lips and raises her hand.

"I enjoyed that very much but I am wondering if you think that if we allow ourselves to look old we may also start acting old?"

Is she saying I look old? How to answer this with tact? My first thought is to point out the obvious, that having no wrinkles, visible pores, or facial movement doesn't make us look young, it makes us look like zombies. I'll refrain from saying that and try to do some good.

"After dying my hair for many years I decided to embrace my silver threads, and while I have a few wrinkles, I feel absolutely content with my appearance. Self-acceptance, confidence, and spirituality helped me achieve so many things and can help anyone who chooses to be optimistic and determined. I am anxious to learn something new every day. That keeps me engaged. It's also important to remember that you can't just live for yourself if you want to stay young in the best possible ways. My best advice is to find a need and fill it. That philosophy helped me author three books and travel world-wide, setting foot on all seven continents. That philosophy brought me to this moment with all of you."

Oh good, she's smiling and nodding as the others clap. In these moments I feel I'm using my gift well.

A slightly rotund woman raises her hand. "I was amazed when you told us your age. You have the physique of a much younger woman. What are your dieting secrets?"

"Thank you for the compliment. I actually weigh less now than I did in my younger days. It has nothing to do with dieting. It has everything to do with lifestyle. I eat healthy foods, including plenty of fruits and vegetables, chicken, turkey, and fish. I also eat yogurt every day and take enzymes as a supplement, because I discovered that my body wasn't producing enough of them. I do not eat red meat, fried foods, or junk food. I may have an occasional piece of chocolate or a cookie, but I seldom eat other pastry. I am very disciplined when I shop. I also exercise at a health club three times a week for approximately 40 to 45 minutes, using a treadmill, bike, rowing machine, leg press, and abdomen rotation machine. The simplest answer, though, is it's about lifestyle. If you are consistent and determined, you can have a better body in your 70s than you had in your 30s."

CHAPTER 16

The bookstore manager indicates there's time for one last question. I decide to call on the elderly gentleman in the front row.

"Thank you for that enlightening talk, ma'am. I don't see a wedding ring on your finger. Can I buy you a cup of coffee after the book signing?"

As the audience erupts into laughter I can't help but think, *It's nice that I continue to get compliments from men.*

"I'm flattered, but I'm a widow and I will never remarry. I have no desire to hook up with anyone new. But it seems there are a bunch of single ladies in the room, so you may get lucky yet," I say with a laugh.

As I sit signing books, women tell me their stories. They tell me about their fears surrounding aging, how they feel discarded by society, and that the image in the mirror doesn't match the image in their minds. I take in each woman's story and try to offer words of compassion and inspiration. "Explore all the facets of your personality," I urge one. "Say this mantra, I am strong and loveable," I tell another. The glimmer in their eyes in each encounter affirms that I am filling a need.

I am like the great oak tree Emmett and I planted in our backyard after we first married. The longer I live, the deeper my roots are planted, grounding me in the fertile soil of wisdom. With each breath I absorb more from my environment, which I transform into oxygen for others. My branches extend ever wider, allowing me to provide more shade.

124

MARNI

59 years old
Heterosexual
Caucasian
Religion listed as "child of the universe"

BREATHE

I met Jonah 12 years ago. I was 48; he was a year younger. We met at a school-related event when I was working on my Ph.D. I attended a workshop that he facilitated. We met four more times at other events, and he hardly took any interest in me—or so it seemed. But at that fifth event, we connected. I knew in that moment that he was the kind of guy I wanted as a life partner. He's cute, warm, wise, funny, and brilliant. My core attraction to Jonah was much deeper. He's spiritually oriented, like I am. I saw the potential to grow together. Both of us have a very deep spiritual foundation. I knew from the beginning that there were very few people who could or would understand the potential for spiritual processes the way he could. I also knew, even before our first date, before he even had a clue who I was, that I would also be that for him. We moved in together four months after we began dating.

Like many people, I had a specific view of what relationships were supposed to be. I saw it perfectly: having our meals together engaged in deep conversation, going out and holding hands, making passionate love. We would be everything to each other. I grew up in dysfunctional relationships and longed for something to help me become whole. I put that on Jonah. For years, I was perpetually disappointed. Jonah did not live up to my expectations. He was not a man of his word. He lacked accountability in regards to time, money, commitments, and agreements. Over and over again, he let me down. Though he talked well of basic spiritual principles, he didn't walk his talk.

What rattled me the most was that he didn't want to spend time with me in the same way I did with him. I wanted to spend as much time as possible together. He barely acknowledged me. I was the last thing on his list of priorities, as if I were less significant than everything else in his life. He was a workaholic, which became a huge sore spot. He didn't turn off his cell during our date time. He didn't sit through dinner without answering the phone. He didn't leave his computer before all the emails were answered and all the newsletters read and explored. I went to bed alone many nights, stewing in resentment. I lost interest in being sexual. Because Jonah wasn't available to me in so many ways—no time, no dates, no hanging out—when he was interested in sex, I felt used. I didn't like that feeling. I became less available and less interested in whether he came to bed with me or not. One night we had a huge fight. After blowing me off to work late, I lay awake in bed fluttering between depression and anger. Eventually I fell asleep. He accidentally woke me up when he came to bed.

"Be quieter. I hate being disturbed in the middle of the night."

"Sorry I woke you, but now that I'm here maybe . . . "

"Are you crazy?!" I screamed as I jumped up. "I have no desire for you whatsoever!"

"That's a shitty thing to say."

"You are not the kind of man I want to make love to. I don't trust you or respect you. You don't treat me as if I matter and am significant."

"The needy, lashing-out thing is bullshit. Maybe I'm not the problem. Maybe you don't respect yourself. Ever think of that?"

"You work all the time, you never have any time for me. Leave me alone. Go fuck your computer."

"That's fucking lovely. I work to give you stability. I'm doing these things so someday I can be more available to you. So fuck you!"

He stormed out and slept on the couch. He didn't speak to me for days, and even though I had been justified, I knew I pushed his buttons and had to apologize. Jonah didn't respond well to emotional ranting or raving. He shut down. I hadn't realized how angry I was until that night. The thing is, over time, resentment turns to rage.

Living together became suffocating—to me, to him, to us. I became consumed by the idea of how a relationship should be, and that sucked the oxygen from everything. With each disappointment my anger grew, leaving less room for anything else. After four years I just couldn't live in the same environment with him. I moved to a different state, but we stayed together, living apart.

When I moved, I knew Jonah and I still had a lot of work to do if we were going to make it work, but I also had an epiphany. I needed to work on myself. This is when I began to own myself again. This is when I began to ask myself the questions that brought clarity.

CHAPTER 17

What would I be doing if I were on my own? How would I want my life to be if I were on my own? I began to live less as a co-dependent woman, trying to create connection in ways that didn't serve me or Jonah. I stopped a lot of the bullshit stuff that "you are supposed to do or have in a relationship" and allowed the relationship to show me what it needed and wanted. This was the beginning of our relationship coming alive again. I gave it room to breathe. I gave Jonah room to breathe. And I gave myself room to breathe, too. Expansion within the relationship began here.

My life has been about expansion in so many ways, and partnership has been the final frontier. It meant literally annihilating an archaic belief system that didn't work for me. When I let go of what a relationship *should* be, many of our conflicts went away. I used to feel like I was settling, but not anymore. Jonah is now a great partner and today we have a really wonderful relationship that we constructed our way.

Ironically, once I let go of the fantasy I got what I had always longed for. Spirituality is about growth, and that is what this relationship has given me. The spiritual role we've played for each other has been the basis for staying in the relationship with him. I've not met anyone, ever, who has the capacity, depth and breadth that Jonah has to understand, allow, and be open to spiritual processes. I really love him: the man, not the fantasy. It's a happily ever after ending—so far.

FURTHER ENGAGEMENT

DISCUSSION OR THOUGHT QUESTIONS

1. Select one woman's story from the book and consider how the story exhibits the concept of low-fat love.
2. Which story stuck out the most to you? Why? What do you think about the woman and her relationship? How do you identify with her, or feel differently than her? What did you learn from her story?
3. Some of the stories portray behaviors the women have engaged in that you may perceive as negative (for example, Sara refusing to speak with her sister, and Kate going through her partner's emails and speaking harshly about his children). Pick one part of a story in which you felt some judgment about the woman's action. Why did you feel that way?
4. Communication is a recurring theme in the women's stories. Select an example that you perceive as unhealthy communication and analyze it.
5. Breaking negative relationship patterns is a central theme in many of the stories. Pick one story in which this occurred. How did the woman change or fail to change destructive patterns? After reading this book, what do you think are the most important things if we seek to improve our relationships with others?
6. Several stories focus on body image and popular culture consumption. What do we learn about pop culture and how it impacts some women from these stories? Offer specific examples.
7. Several images appear as symbols throughout the stories: for example, mirrors. Select one of these recurring images and consider its meaning in the women's lives, literally and metaphorically.
8. Some of the women express feeling like a fraud (for example, Valerie and Jane). This recalls what bell hooks (2000) has written about in terms of the importance of authenticity for building self-esteem, as discussed in the Introduction. What do you think about this issue?

9. What do you think first-person narration added to the stories? How might the stories be different if written in the third-person?
10. How might this book be different if it focused on men's stories of low-fat love? What role does gender play in the stories in the book?

CREATIVE WRITING EXERCISES

1. Select one of the stories and rewrite it from the perspective of the person the woman has a relationship with. For example, how might Kayla's former girlfriend write their story?
2. Rewrite one of the stories using third-person narration. Consider how you might describe the setting, the activities the characters are engaged in, and how you might offer commentary on the main character and the relationships portrayed.
3. Select a relationship you have experienced, past or present, that you consider "dissatisfying." Write your story. Give yourself a pseudonym and write it as fiction, if that makes it easier.
4. Write an open letter to one of the women featured in this book. What would you say to her to offer your empathy or advice?
5. Consider Leala and Valerie: Note the similarities in Valerie and Leala's relationship patterns. If they ever met, what might these two women say to each other? Write a dialogue.

QUALITATIVE RESEARCH ACTIVITIES

1. Collect a small sample of pop culture representations, inspired by those in the book (for example, the fashion magazines Yael reads; the reality TV, entertainment TV, websites or music videos Jane watches; or the media featuring the "plus size" celebrities Keisha admires). Conduct a qualitative content analysis.
2. Select several scenes of dialogue from this book, or use Mary and Eleanor's story "Mirror Mirror" and perform discourse or conversation analysis on the dialogue.

ARTISTIC EXERCISES

1. *Yael*. Read Yael's story and look at the portrait. Note the difference between what she says in her interview and how she really feels about herself. Imagine she designs a T-shirt that she is comfortable wearing. Design a T-shirt using the template below. Use markers, pens, or colored pencils, and feel free to use words as well.

2. *Jane*. Select a women's magazine of your choice. Find a full body image of a woman that you think reflects Jane's ideal body image. Cut and paste it here.

Discuss the beauty standards in our society reflected in the image.

3. *Emma*. Browse through magazines or search online for a portrait of a well-known person. Think how this person has been labeled (in the media, by peers, boss, etc.). Cut and paste the portrait to roughly fit the outline provided. On the dotted line on the necklace, write a label that you think has been attributed to this person. Feel free to add more necklaces! Discuss how the person is feeling.

4. *Emma* (Part Two). Find a picture of yourself. Think about how you have been labeled (by peers, your boss/colleagues, romantic partner, parents, teachers, etc.). Cut and paste the picture to roughly fit the outline provided. On the dotted line on the necklace, write a label that you think has been attributed to you. Feel free to add more necklaces! Discuss how this makes you feel.

A CONVERSATION ABOUT THE METHOD
USED IN THIS BOOK

Patricia: Inspired by the stories readers shared with me in response to my novel *Low-Fat Love*, I conducted a new set of interviews, explicitly seeking women who had experienced a dissatisfying relationship or who wanted to speak about their relationship with their own bodies. I had such a large response rate to the recruitment notices I circulated that I eventually had to turn potential interviewees away. I think that speaks to how many women want an opportunity to share their relationship and body stories and don't have a safe outlet. I had never conducted interview research by email before, but it worked well in this situation because it enabled me to include women from all over the United States with very different backgrounds. Given the sensitive subject matter, I also think it allowed the women the opportunity to reflect on their lives, and to use the language they wanted to use to express their experiences. Once I had collected all the completed interviews, I sought a book contract from my publisher for *Low-Fat Love Stories*, intending to write a traditional monograph based on the interview research.

I immersed myself in the data, engaged in multiple rounds of analysis and interpretation, and attempted to outline the book. Every time I began to write, I got stuck. The writing felt stale and I feared I wasn't doing justice to the essence of the women's stories. I put the project on the back burner several times and worked on other things, hoping that when I returned to it, inspiration would strike. Each time I returned to the project I hit the same wall. For the first time in my career I was entirely blocked.

Victoria Scotti then contacted me. We had met previously at a conference and had mutual colleagues. At the time, Victoria was completing her doctorate in creative arts therapy. Her university required a 10-month practicum experience and she asked if she could work for me as a research assistant. Victoria is a talented visual artist and a scholar with expertise in arts-based research, one of my primary areas of interest. For those unfamiliar, arts-based research (ABR) is an approach to research that involves adapting the tenets of the creative arts in social research projects across the disciplines (please see my book *Method Meets Art: Arts-Based Research Practice, Second Edition* for a detailed discussion). I gladly agreed to work with Victoria. During a Skype session she told me more about the interview research she planned to conduct with women for her dissertation. It made me think of *Low-Fat Love Stories*. I told her about the interview research I conducted and how I wasn't quite sure what to do with it. She suggested that I send her some of it.

At that point I had created summaries of each of the interviews. The summaries were two to three pages single-spaced, and included demographic information, the focus of the interview, keywords, the major themes, and numerous excerpts (the quotes I thought stood out and captured the different themes in each interview). I sent her a couple of summaries and she emailed me back, "When I read these, I see portraits." We developed an idea for how to proceed with the book.

My expertise is in fiction as a research practice, fiction-based research (FBR), or social fiction, all terms I have coined in my work over the years. This approach to research employs literary writing in service of social research purposes. So I knew that I would draw on this skill set in some capacity, but I didn't know exactly what form my writing would take until Victoria responded to the first interview summary and our method developed.

Victoria: I'm an art therapist, artist, and arts-based researcher. When I was working on my Ph.D., an opportunity came up to work with Patricia Leavy, and I was thrilled. Although Patricia is not an art therapist, I knew of her long-term support for and deep understanding of the creative arts therapies. Patricia's books had inspired my passion for arts-based research, and I was hoping that this could be an opportunity for an interdisciplinary collaboration. When Patricia presented the project to me, and asked if I could help her with it by offering a different perspective, I couldn't believe my ears. It doesn't happen every day that an experienced writer and researcher seeks and values a graduate student's perspective. She believed in me and trusted me from the start, which was incredibly humbling. What was so amazing about working with her was that Patricia was completely open, and she trusted me and my expertise in the visual modality and what I had to offer. She never imposed any boundaries on me.

The only limitation we had from the start was that the artwork had to be black and white for publishing reasons (although I also used red in the initial visual concepts). My only concern was that Patricia would not be able to accept my renderings of the women, which might be drastically different than what they actually look like. I was relieved to learn she had conducted the interviews via email and thus didn't know what the women look like, either. This freed me. We knew the creation of this book would be an iterative process and collaboration. In ABR, often times, the process of analysis and representation is iterative and can involve several phases that build on each other. In this project, the visual and the text respond to each other.

When Patricia sent me the initial concepts and direct quotes, I was immediately struck by the honesty with which the women shared their stories, and the depth of the emotion. Using the women's direct words was so powerful; it felt like they were confessing their stories to me. I felt trusted and privileged. I felt that the women had a need to tell their stories, to be heard and seen. The first participant that Patricia sent me was Kayla, and after taking in the data, I felt in my body the pain and suffering that she was going through, so it was a visceral experience for me. To embody the woman's data, I took the pose of the woman, letting my own body guide me to create a body pose for her. Embodying the woman helped me envision her facial expression. It was clear that the raw data had a powerful visceral effect on me, but how could I transmit this to others, first to Patricia? I drew from my training and experience as an art therapist. In art therapy practice, art therapists often experience visceral reactions in response to their clients. In order to process these reactions and feelings, art therapists work through difficult client cases in supervision. In supervision, art therapists' own art-making forms an integral part of the expression and communication. Sometimes, art therapists envision being in the client's position, or respond to their work with the client using artistic expression. In my experience, I have often created an image of what it might feel like to be the client. These images have helped me gain insight about and build empathy with the client, and also helped me communicate my experiences to the supervisor and peers.

In this project, I realized that using portraiture might be a way to communicate these visceral experiences first to Patricia, and ultimately to others as well, and so I started with the "visual concept." This became a portrait sketch that I created after reading and contemplating the raw data. I used a sketchbook to create the visual concepts. I worked with each woman's data, separately. I wrote memos about the data, including my own emotional reactions to the data as well as any visions that came up for me. The memos also included sketches in response to the data. Then I made several quick sketches that I finally elaborated into the visual concept. The original concept sketches were made in pencil and I also wrote one or two quotes that particularly stood out to me. The goal of this phase was to express to Patricia the visceral experience that the participant's data evoked in me.

Patricia: When Victoria sent me the "visual concept" for Kayla, the first story we worked on, I was immediately drawn into Kayla's world in a new way. The way the themes in the interview intertwined in the visual image spoke to me like a short story, or a series of layered "snapshots." I decided to adopt a short story format, although it was a new genre for me. I immediately felt the stories had to be told in the first-person, although that was also a new approach for me and I had some trepidation. I wanted the women to be able to communicate their stories through Victoria's pencil and ink, and through my storytelling. They are the narrators, through our filters. Once I had the genre and narrator point-of-view determined, I knew how to proceed.

Victoria sent me a "visual concept" and I meditated on it, sometimes just for minutes and other times for weeks. Each one blew me away and provided me a new way to think about the woman's story. I knew from the start we were working on something exciting that was opening up new meanings. When I was ready to write,

I placed the visual in front of me at my desk and I took out the woman's verbatim interview transcript. Drawing inspiration from the visual, I wrote each woman's story, using exact language from her interview transcript whenever possible. During the writing process, I put my words in black ink and language taken directly from the transcript in red ink so we'd have a record of my language and their language. On average, the stories are about half the woman's own language and half mine. There is variation, though, with some stories using 20–80% of their precise language. I believe each story accurately reflects the interview it is meant to represent. Regardless of whose language I used, I held complete fidelity to the themes and topics in the interviews. For example, if childhood abuse is a theme in an interview, it is a theme in the story. I also was true to the details in the interview transcripts, such as people's ages, specific mentions of popular culture, food items, weight, and so forth. Metaphors and symbols that appear in the stories, such as images from fairytales and the omnipresence of mirrors, were all directly developed out of the interviews. I employed artistic license only to create scenes or situations, such as memories and dialogue. However, these scenes or situations were used as devices to directly communicate information from the interviews. While each story is in short form and told from a first-person perspective, I had other decisions to make for each story, as well. For example, some include dialogue and interiority, while others do not; some are presented in specific formats, such as diary entries or a conversation; and some unfold in one day whereas others are series of memories over many years. When each story was drafted I sent it to Victoria.

Victoria: When I read Patricia's stories, I felt that I had the privilege to be let into someone else's world. The stories were so powerful, often times I had goosebumps and was even moved to tears. This mirrored the feelings I've experienced in art therapy practice when I meet with clients face to face and they open up about the things they've never told anyone before. Reading Patricia's writing was a very similar experience. When I saw how Patricia used my visual concept, how my images were mirrored in the stories, I was in awe. This is when I realized that these "textual-visual snapshots" are pieces that come together as one. We had created a method that allowed for each of our expertise in the arts to come together through an iterative collaborative process. For me it was an experience of growth. Having that other modality really opens up a different world and you can see how it can only enrich your own work. The purpose of this project, as it is arts-based research, is to communicate an aspect of somebody's life to the reader or the viewers who otherwise would not have access to this information and these experiences. As Patricia has emphasized many times, it is difficult for lay audiences to access and understand academic papers. However, through this form of representation, these experiences can become alive and anyone can engage with them. Whenever I've taught undergraduate and graduate courses, and presented at conferences, I've found that the students really relate to the more artful representations of research findings, including the visual representations. Through this project, I see how we can bridge the visual and the textual forms of representation, and also create pieces that can be used both by academic and lay audiences. I believe that these "textual-visual snapshots" can be quite powerful for student and lay audiences alike. ABR allows us to invite others into the experiences of each woman, through which many people's experiences are communicated. This is how you can relate and get a more personal perspective and understanding of what is going on for many women in terms of relationships and body image.

Patricia: This collaborative process was not only joyful for me, but also opened up new ways for me to see and think about interview research and representation. From a writing perspective, this was also a huge challenge. While I have written several novels as well as many nonfiction books, I have never written in the first-person, nor have I written in any kind of short story format. I was amazed by how much it would sometimes take to write so little in terms of word count. It was a wonderful challenge. While the stories are quite short, many of them carry years or decades of experiences, some beginning in childhood. Having come to know these interview transcripts, as well as the stories of the interviewees we did not directly represent in this book, over a period of years, I truly believe the visual art and text in this book captures the heart of what these women shared with me.

Victoria: Yes, I agree, to me these "textual-visual snapshots" are concise but powerful representations of the women's experiences. I think that from the methods perspective, there is a fit between the short story format and the portrait format. It allows readers to have a multi-dimensional impact from witnessing these stories. The fit is due to the fact that by looking at the portrait, you can take in their experiences, and by reading the stories, they reinforce each other. Each case is short but emotionally laden and I think, powerful.

The portrait format and the short story go hand in hand. By depicting facial expressions, I can depict the emotions, they can be "read," because we relate to each other through facial expressions. But also, portraiture is a genre that can be stretched or extended from just the outside representation so that I was also able to include in these portraits some aspects of the person that are invisible to the eye but nevertheless form a part who this person is. For instance, the fantasies or haunting past experiences that the women talked about.

The final portrait that followed was more elaborate, and made in pen and ink. The purpose of the final portrait was to mirror the story. As I mentioned earlier, the black and white color scheme was chosen because of the publishing limitations (we did not want the book to become cost prohibitive for readers).

There is also something to be said here about relationality. As Patricia mentioned, many women see themselves relationally. In the interviews, when the women talk about their relationship with the other person, they say as much about the other person as they say about themselves. So I realized that the other person became a part of the portrait, like a shadow. Sometimes they haunted the protagonist like a shadow. This made me represent the "other" in the portrait as well, because we cannot look at the women in isolation from their past experiences, their relationships, and their bodies. They are tightly intertwined. For instance, one symbol that is present throughout the book is a rope (represented in many portraits). The women were tied in with the other, sometimes they were able to cut the rope, and other times not. This symbolically stands for low-fat love, something that you settle for.

Patricia: I think it's important to mention that originally Victoria signed on as a research assistant to this project. However, by the time we had drafted the art and text for two of the women, it was clear to me that Victoria was, in fact, a co-author. She was not an illustrator, but a co-author. Neither the images or text in this book could have been created without the other. It was a completely iterative process, and both the images and text are of equal importance. With her permission, I contacted my publisher to alter my book contract accordingly. As an arts-based researcher I think it's important to point this out for two reasons. First, if we value each art form equally, this needs to be reflected in how we name what we have done and assign credit. I felt strongly that Victoria's name needed to be on the book as an author. Second, if we value each art form equally, we need to think seriously about compensation. This is a part of ethical practice. Often practitioners engaged in non-text-based forms of artful inquiry are not compensated equally to those engaged in literary practices. Likewise, graduate students are often improperly credited and compensated for their scholarly contributions. By changing my book contract to reflect Victoria as a co-author, she was entitled to equal compensation. We feel this has material and symbolic consequences of import and hope others in the field use it as a model for how collaboration within or across artistic forms might proceed.

Because I have collaborated many times over the years, to varying degrees of success, and this collaboration was truly special, I want to say a few words about why I think it worked so well. Victoria and I had a mutual trust and respect for one another. I gave her free rein as a visual artist, and she afforded me the same as a writer. It's important that when you bring other experts into the mix you really utilize them to their full potential. That takes trust and freedom. We both had that throughout this process. While we did respond to each other's work (for example, saying what we thought worked well and sharing our own personal responses to what the other created) we did not try to micromanage each other or influence the other's creative process. We were open to what the other would create. I think that as much as we respect each other, we also respect the nature of creativity.

We were also flexible from day one. Even after we developed our methodology, we always said that if it stopped working, meaning doing justice to the women's interviews, we would regroup and adapt. We were also flexible with our work schedules. We each had other projects going on and had to put this one aside for a few weeks or months at a time throughout the process. We had the attitude that it would be done when it was done, and there was no need to force it.

Victoria: I'm humbled by Patricia's generosity and acknowledgment of my work. More than anything, I'm in awe of Patricia's openness to reach out, be fearless, and trust me throughout this journey that we traveled together for more than two years. I believe that collaborations have a huge potential in ABR because we can join forces and pool the strengths of different art forms to more fully express the participants' experiences. In our case, it was short stories and visual portraits, but these collaborations could be fostered, and indeed have been done, across different genres such as music and the visual arts, dance and music, etc. Hopefully our example will inspire other scholars across disciplines to seek new ways of collaboration, because I believe that they can be enriching to both.

Final words from us both: We wanted this book to be useful for general readers, in courses across disciplines, and for qualitative and arts-based researchers and students. With the latter in mind, we created this appendix and we also include our interview guides in Appendix B.

We are aware that in ABR, the processes of data analysis and representation sometimes remain elusive. By presenting the different stages of data generation, analysis, and representation, we attempt to make this process transparent. We hope that our method can inspire others to conduct their own ABR studies, or adapt our method to suit a variety of needs. We want to take this opportunity to briefly summarize our methodology, noting that in practice the phases of data analysis and representation overlapped. Here are the phases of research for developing "textual-visual snapshots:"

1. Recruiting research participants and obtaining informed consent
2. Data generation (interviews)
3. Qualitative data analysis (Patricia)
4. Iterative data generation and visual analysis (Victoria, visual concept)
5. Iterative arts-based data analysis and literary representation (Patricia, final story)
6. Iterative arts-based data analysis and visual representation (Victoria, final portrait)

Please note that the final stories and final portraits were drafted and revised, often numerous times.

THE INTERVIEW GUIDES

Romantic Relationship Interview: Dissatisfying Relationships

Thank you for sharing your story. The more detailed you are in the following interview the better I will understand and be able to express your story. So please share as much information as possible (stories and examples are great). Your emotions—how people and events have made you feel, how you have come to terms with these issues, and how you make sense of them, are particularly important. There are no right and wrong answers; I want to hear *your* story. Not all of the info you share will be included in the book, but it will help me to write your story. Please feel free to skip any questions that make you uncomfortable or are not applicable to your situation. Also, please feel free to address any issues that you feel I omitted or are important to understanding your interview responses. Please take your time and submit the typed interview and interview release (allowing me to publish your story) within four weeks. If you need more time please let me know. Thank you again!

Contact Information (for internal use only)

Full Name:
Current Age:
Location:
E-Mail:
Mailing Address:
Occupation:
Sexual Orientation (Optional):
Race or Ethnicity (Optional):
Religion (Optional):

Background

Is this a current or past relationship?
What is/was the length of this relationship?
Any on-again, off-again periods? If so, please explain.
Was or is this an exclusive relationship? Please explain.

> If this was/is an exclusive relationship, were/are there any issues of infidelity? If yes, please explain.

Were/are you married or legally partnered to this person?
Have you ever lived together? If so, do you still live together?
How did you meet?

The Relationship

How would you describe this relationship? (Please explain)
What attracted you to this person?
What do you most like/love about him/her? Why?
What do you most dislike about him/her?
Has this person disappointed you, or failed to live up to your expectations?

> If so, how?

Was the relationship ever primarily positive, or was it always difficult in some way? Please explain.
What would you say the primary problems in the relationship are/were?
Describe the aspect(s) of this relationship that made you feel badly.
During the course of this relationship, have you had to look the other way or make excuses for bad behavior from this person?

> If so, please offer an example and explain how this makes you feel.

What does this person do that is hurtful or upsetting? Any specific examples or stories?
How do you respond to these situations?
Has there been any physical abuse in the relationship? If so, please explain.

Has there been any sexual abuse in the relationship? If so, please explain.

Has there been any emotional or psychological abuse in the relationship? If so, please explain.

Has there been any financial abuse in the relationship? If so, please explain.

How do you express your feelings to this person?

How do they generally treat you? Any specific examples or stories?

How do you treat him/her?

How do you speak to each other? (Tone, level of honesty, etc.)

Have there been any issues of jealousy, insecurity, and/or obsession in this relationship?

    If so, explain.

Does this person bring out the best or worst in you? Please explain.

When in this relationship do you feel your life shrinking or expanding? Please explain.

How do you resolve conflict with each other?

How do you express anger toward each other?

How would you characterize your physical/sexual relationship? Please explain.

How important was/is the physical/sexual aspect of this relationship to you?

What, if any, aspect(s) of this person/relationship do you like? Please explain.

How important is this/was this relationship to you? Why?

How much of your identity do you feel is linked to this relationship? Why?

Do you feel like you are settling (or have settled) in this relationship?

    If so, how? Why?

Why do you think you stayed in/maintained this relationship?

If you are no longer seeing this person, please explain how the relationship ended.

    How did this make you feel?

    How do you feel now when you think about this person?

Do you share friends in common with this person?

If so, how has that impacted you?

Have you discussed this relationship with others?

If so, what did they say?

What do you think your role is/was in creating this dissatisfying relationship?

What, if anything, will you do differently in this or other relationships in the future?

What has this relationship taught you about yourself?

What has this relationship taught you about relationships?

Has this relationship impacted other romantic relationships? If so, how?

What would be your ideal relationship?

How would that ideal relationship differ from this dissatisfying one?

Have you been able to achieve your ideal relationship with a different person? Please explain.

Have you had other similarly dissatisfying relationships with other men/women? Please explain.

If so, would you consider this a pattern?

Anything else you would like to add?

Thank you, thank you, thank you! I look forward to reading your interview and writing about your experience. I am honored that you have taken the time to share your story.

Family Interview: Dissatisfying Relationships

Same intro and contact info section.

Background

What is your relationship to this person (for example, mother, sister, cousin, etc.)?

Have you ever lived in the same household as this person? If so, when? Do you still?

If you do not live in the same household (at this time) how often do you see each other?

Has there ever been any physical, sexual and/or emotional/ psychological abuse in this relationship? If so, please explain.

The Relationship

How would you describe this relationship? Please explain in detail.
What is it about this relationship that you are dissatisfied with?
When did difficulty begin in this relationship? Please explain.
Describe the aspect(s) of this relationship that made/make you feel badly.
During the course of this relationship, have you had to look the other way or make excuses for bad behavior from this person?
> If so, please offer an example and explain how this makes you feel.
What does this person do that is hurtful or upsetting? Any specific examples or stories?
How do you respond to these situations?
How do you express your feelings to this person?
How do they generally treat you? Any specific examples or stories?
How do you treat him/her?
How do you speak to each other? (Tone, level of honesty, etc.)
How do you resolve conflict with each other?
How do you express anger toward each other?
What, if any, aspect(s) of this person/relationship do you like? Please explain.
How important is or was this relationship to you? Why?
How much of your identity do you feel is linked to this relationship? Why?
Do you feel like you have had to put up with this relationship only because it is with a family member? If so, please explain how this makes you feel.
If you no longer see this person, please explain if there was an argument or some other event?
How do you feel now when you think about this person and your family?
How has your relationship with this person impacted other family members? Please explain.
How, if at all, has this relationship impacted you on holidays and/or family occasions? Please explain.

Do you have a spouse or partner?

> If so, how has your relationship with your family member impacted your spouse/partner?

Have you discussed this relationship with others in your family?

> If so, what did they say?

Do you have other similarly dissatisfying, relationships with other members of your family? Please explain.

What do you think your role is in creating this dissatisfying relationship?

What has this relationship taught you about yourself?

What has this relationship taught you about relationships?

What would be your ideal relationship with this person?

How would that ideal relationship differ from this dissatisfying one?

Anything else you would like to add?

Thank you, thank you, thank you! I look forward to reading your interview and writing about your experience. I am honored that you have taken the time to share your story.

Body Image and Identity Interview

Same intro and contact info section.

Overview

Please tell me, in as much detail as you can provide, how you feel about your appearance. (Physical features, hair, body, weight, skin, etc.)

Overall, would you say that you are mostly satisfied or mostly dissatisfied with your appearance?

Do you have a history of weight gain/loss? If so, please explain.

Have you ever had, or do you have, an eating disorder (compulsive overeating, anorexia, bulimia)?

> If so, please explain (what, when, for how long, etc.).

Appearance Satisfaction

What, if anything, do you like about your appearance? Please explain.
How does this make you feel?

Appearance Dissatisfaction

What, if anything, do you dislike about your appearance? Please explain.

How does this make you feel?

How long have you felt this way?

Do you remember why you started feeling this way? Please explain.

Is this important to you? If so, why?

How often do you think about the things you dislike about your appearance?

How much of your identity, if any, is linked to this dissatisfaction?

What, if anything, do you do to try and change this? Please explain.

How, if at all, does this impact your relationships?

How, if at all, does this impact your sexuality?

How, if at all, does this impact your confidence? Please explain (for example, is this uniformly the case, or does it occur in certain contexts?)

Diet and Exercise

Please describe your eating habits (what kinds of foods do you eat, do you do your own grocery shopping, do you cook, do you eat out a lot, do you mainly eat alone or with others, do you follow a particular diet, etc.).

How do you feel after you eat? Please explain any guilt or other negative feelings?

Please describe your exercise habits and/or athleticism (if applicable).

Personal Style

Please describe your personal style.

What three words best categorize your personal style?

What does your style say about you? (What does it reflect about your personality, values or interests?)

How typically "feminine" do you consider your style? Please explain.

What kind of clothes/fashion do you normally wear?

Is how you dress linked to your work life? If so, please explain.

Do you dress differently in different areas of your life? If so, please explain.

Are there things you would like to try (clothing styles, hairstyles, etc.) that you don't? If so, why not?

Do you think women can get stuck in a certain look without exploring other parts of their personalities?

> If so, have you experienced this?

> If so, please explain.

Pop Culture

How much mainstream pop culture do you typically consume daily? (Television viewing, movies, magazines, etc.)

How do you think pop culture (TV, movies, magazines) depicts women? (Beauty, body ideal, roles)

How does this make you feel?

Do you feel personally impacted?

> If so, how?

Do you think pop culture portrays women in stereotyped ways?

> If so, can you offer any examples?

> If so, do you think that impacts women's identity? How so?

What, if any, changes would you like to see in how pop culture portrays women?

Anything else you would like to add?

Thank you, thank you, thank you! I look forward to reading your interview and writing about your experience. I am honored that you have taken the time to share your story.

ABOUT THE AUTHORS

Patricia Leavy, Ph.D., is an independent scholar (formerly Associate Professor of Sociology, Chair of Sociology & Criminology and Founding Director of Gender Studies at Stonehill College). She is widely considered an international leader in the fields of qualitative and arts-based research. As an author, she has earned critical and commercial success in both nonfiction and fiction. Her twenty-one published books include *Method Meets Art: Arts-Based Research Practice* (Guilford Press, first and second editions), *The Oxford Handbook of Qualitative Research* (Oxford University Press), *Fiction as Research Practice* (Left Coast Press/Routledge), *Essentials of Transdisciplinary Research* (Left Coast Press/Routledge) and the bestselling novels *Low-Fat Love* (Sense Publishers, first and second editions), *American Circumstance* (Sense Publishers, first and second editions) and *Blue* (Sense Publishers). Her work is being translated into multiple languages. She is also series creator and editor of seven book series with Oxford University Press and Sense Publishers, including the ground-breaking *Social Fictions* series. Known for her commitment to public scholarship, she is frequently called on by the US national news media and has regular blogs for *The Huffington Post, The Creativity Post,* and *We Are the Real Deal.* She has received numerous career awards, including the New England Sociological Association 2010 New England Sociologist of the Year Award, the American Creativity Association 2014 Special Achievement Award, the American Educational Research Association Qualitative SIG 2015 Egon Guba Memorial Keynote Lecture Award, and the International Congress of Qualitative Inquiry 2015 Special Career Award (she is the youngest recipient). In 2016, Mogul, a global women's empowerment network, named Leavy an "Influencer" along with Chelsea Clinton, Melissa Etheridge, Nina Garcia, and other notable women. Her first article for Mogul was their number one trending piece worldwide the week it was released, read by more than 17,000 people. Her website is www.patricialeavy.com.

Victoria Scotti, Ph.D., is an art therapist, artist, independent arts-based researcher, and a lecturer. Her multidisciplinary work centers around women's lived experiences, which she investigates from the perspectives of art therapy, the fine arts, and arts-based research. She recently graduated from Drexel University, Philadelphia (USA), with a Ph.D. in Creative Arts Therapies, and her doctoral dissertation was entitled *Beyond words: Making meaning of transitioning to motherhood using montage portraiture*. A native of Estonia, Victoria Scotti shares her time between Spain, Estonia, and USA, and she is committed to collaborations across disciplines and internationally. Her website is www.victoriascotti.com.

CPSIA information can be obtained
at www.ICGtesting.com
Printed in the USA
FSOW04n1724271016
26607FS

9 789463 008167